JAGUAR XJ

THE COMPLETE COMPANION

NIGEL THORLEY

BAY VIEW BOOKS

Published 1991 by
Bay View Books Ltd
13a Bridgeland Street
Bideford, Devon EX39 2QE

© Bay View Books Ltd 1991

Reprinted 1992

Designed by Gerrard Lindley
Typeset by Lens Typesetting, Bideford

ISBN 1 870979 22 2

Printed in Hong Kong

Acknowledgements

In the preparation of this book there have been so many people and organisations who have assisted me in the collation of facts, figures, photographs and other information that it would be impossible to thank them all in the space provided. I would however like to thank certain people personally for their unstinting support in spite of continual badgering and pestering from me to provide information necessary to complete this work.

Firstly I must thank all at Jaguar Cars in Coventry: Director Colin Cooke, Chief Photographer Roger Clinkscales, Ian Luckett, and the staff in the Publications Department, for allowing me the space and time to work through the service records.

Particular thanks must go to Ken Jenkins, Technical Adviser to the Jaguar Enthusiasts' Club, who checked out many of the facts and figures I had written; his amazing knowledge of all things Jaguar I don't think can be bettered anywhere.

To the many others who provided information or lent cars for photography and tests, I offer my very sincere thanks.

I am grateful to my publisher Charles Herridge for having faith in me to produce this work, for giving me his support and for his patience when I was late in producing the copy.

Finally, I must thank my wife Pauline, who has always been so understanding during the long hours when I was locked away in the study typing!

Contents

Introduction

The late Sir Williams Lyons, co-founder of Jaguar and at the helm of the Company through the introduction of the XJ Series.

Sir John Egan, the man who put Jaguar back on its feet in the eighties, rekindling the early success of the XJ Series.

The name of Jaguar has long been synonymous with fine luxury saloons as well as sports cars. Whilst it is not the purpose of this book to retrace the history of the marque — ground already covered many times in other publications — to set the scene for the models dealt with in this book it is necessary quickly to recall the background to Jaguar's saloon car range leading up to the introduction of the XJ Series. Although the story of Jaguar dates back to the Swallow Sidecar Company in Blackpool, and William Lyons' adaptation of the Austin Seven with sleek two-tone bodywork, the saloon car heritage really started with the SS 1½- and 2½-litre four-door models introduced in September 1935, based around Standard mechanicals. These cars, along with the later 3½-litre version introduced in September 1937, continued the Lyons theme of excellent value for money and superb styling. At the public unveiling of the SS Jaguar saloon in 1935 at the Mayfair Hotel in London, no one could guess the price of the new model and there was astonishment when Lyons announced that it would be sold at an unbelievably low £395! With a total production of around 20,000 up to 1949 these cars were the foundation of Jaguar's success.

There followed the Mark V, a developed version of the previous SS Jaguars with better streamlining, the soon-to-be-familiar full rear wheel spats, lots of brightwork and, for the first time on a Jaguar, independent front suspension. From 1948 to 1951 only 10,500 were produced — but this was an interim model whilst the Mark VII saloon was under development. Before leaving this era of Jaguar saloon car manufacture it is worth mentioning that the Mark V was the last Jaguar saloon to be available in drophead two-door form, and the last Jaguar saloon to be available with two-door coachwork until the introduction of the XJ Coupé.

The Mark VII saloon (the Mark VI designation was never used to avoid conflict with a Bentley model of the period) was released in October 1950. It was an "all new" model with beautifully sleek four-door coachwork of genuine North American proportions, independent front suspension, and ride and comfort levels never before seen in a car at such a competitive price. Most importantly the Mark VII featured the newly developed XK six-cylinder twin overhead camshaft engine specially designed for this new large saloon but previously released in the XK120 sports car. The Mark VII was motoring in the truly British grand style, a car that took the world by storm and remained in production in various guises (Mark VIIM, VIII

The SS Airline coupé, whose two-door pillarless construction was echoed in the XJ Coupé.

and IX) up to 1961 with a total production run of around 47,200. This model range more than any other established Jaguar as one of the leading manufacturers of luxury saloons. Jaguar's Mark VII advertising slogan proudly announced that these excellent cars had "Grace ... Space ... and Pace" — a maxim that has remained true to this day of all Jaguar's large saloons.

Despite the success of the Mark VII, VIII and IX, by 1961 there was no doubt that their styling was becoming dated, particularly where the valued North American market was concerned. And so in October 1961 Jaguar announced the new Mark X saloon, utilising a 3.8-litre version of the XK engine with no less than three SU carburettors. Flagship of the Jaguar range, the Mark X was really up to date, with fully independent front and rear suspension incorporating the E Type-style rear subframe with a wider track and a very high degree of interior comfort. Although quite "modern", the Mark X still had the traditional leather and wood veneer, even picnic tables in the backs of the front seats. The body style was certainly a conversation piece: you either loved it or hated it. Low slung and purposeful, the Mark X carried on the Jaguar tradition of Grace, Space and Pace and remains the longest Jaguar production saloon ever, at 16ft 10in. It also has the dubious honour of being the widest British production car ever, at 6ft 4in!

Although it initially met with mixed reactions there is no doubt that the Mark X was successful in its own right, remaining in production until August 1970 after modification to a 4.2-litre engine and later to 420G designation with minor cosmetic changes. Total production amounted to some 24,280 cars (including limousine versions), and the model actually remained in production after the introduction of the XJ series, running alongside the XJ until sales slumped and the extra production capacity was needed to expand XJ6 output.

The Mark X/420G saloon, flagship of the range in the mid-sixties and predecessor to the XJ6 and the one-model policy.

The Mark X/420G model also formed the basis of the Daimler DS420 limousine, hand-made specifically for Royalty, Heads of State and the carriage trade. Initially produced at Browns Lane, then at the Vanden Plas coachworks in London, and subsequently moved back to Coventry, it is still in production at the time of writing.

The demise of the 420G brings the story up to the point when Jaguar launched its one model policy with the introduction on 26th September 1968 of the XJ Series 1 saloon in 2.8-litre and 4.2-litre forms. Prior to this date Jaguar had been producing a vast and varied range of saloons including 240, 340, 3.4-litre S Type, 3.8-litre S Type, 420 and 420G saloon and limousine, *plus* the Daimler derivatives of the above models, V8 250 and 420 Sovereign — a total of no less than eight different models based around four body styles and two distinct engine types not including the Daimler DS420 limousine.

With the introduction of the XJ Series 1 Jaguar immediately dropped the following from the range: 340, 420, 3.4-litre S Type, 3.8-litre S type and 420G limousine. The Daimler versions soldiered on until the introduction of the Daimler XJ Sovereigns, the 240 until April 1969 and the 420G (saloon) until August 1970, by which time Jaguar had achieved their aim of producing one basic body shell in various guises to suit different markets. The XJ was here to stay and stay it has, although production is now much reduced: the XJ Series III in V12 form is now one of the most exclusive saloons in the world with a total production of less than 2,000 per year.

The XJ series has seen the Jaguar company through the good times of the late sixties and early seventies, the decline of the marque and the period of BL ownership, and back to its current acclaimed position under the leadership of Sir John Egan and now Ford.

"Enter the Private World of the Jaguar XJ6"

The first full-colour brochure for the XJ6 proclaimed these words in its introduction to what was one of the most important new models produced by Jaguar in its history.

"The new Jaguar sedan is going to be quickly recognised as one of the world's best-balanced cars" (*Car and Driver* magazine). "So subtle, so English — Jaguar's XJ6"(*Car* magazine). "The sound of silence . . . best British car of the decade . . . the XJ6 sets difficult-to-match standards" (*Modern Motor* magazine). "British and Best, the latest Jaguar sets impressive new standards . . . combination of performance, comfort, roadholding and quietness unrivalled at the price" (*Motor* magazine). These were just a few of the many accolades given to the new XJ Jaguar saloons on their introduction to the public in October 1968. The fact that the XJ Series has remained in production longer than any other Jaguar saloon is testimony in itself to the sound engineering and brilliant styling conceived in the Lyons mould, but what led up to its birth and to the decision to use it to replace so many other models?

The XJ6's immediate predecessor, the Mark X/420G, had by 1968 been in production for only seven years, and although its styling had not been considered wholly successful the car was still relatively modern in concept and design. The employment of modern technology in the form of all independent suspension and monocoque construction combined with advanced styling had kept the model ahead of such competition as the Rover 3-litre and Humber Imperial in this country; it was cheaper and better equipped than equivalent Mercedes in Europe; and in North America it was a far more roadworthy package than the home grown Cadillacs, Lincolns and the like. Yet, recognising the necessity of rationalising models and having a car ready to accept the challenge of the seventies, Jaguar decided to develop an entirely new model, which nevertheless would use the technology and structural strength of the Mark X/420G to the best advantage.

The 420G was not very economical to run, had somewhat oversoft suspension, offered poor lateral support for driver and passenger, was excessively wide, and was endowed with exceptionally bulbous styling — but having said all that the car was built with the North American market in mind! The XJ6, however, would put all these matters right, with a lot more besides.

The XJ6 was released to the public on 26th September 1968 in time for the British Motor Show of that year; other new models produced around the same time included the all new Ford Escort, the Vauxhall FD Victor, the Sunbeam Rapier fastback, the MGC, the Austin 3-litre and the Triumph 2.5 PI. None of these outshone the Jaguar, which was subsequently to be voted Car of the Year by *Car* magazine, a unanimous decision by fifteen panelists from seven countries.

Over £6 million had been invested in the development of the XJ6 since 1964. It was to be the most important and technically advanced car that Jaguar had ever built. The new saloon bore a definite and intended family resemblance to other Jaguar saloons, and although conceived as a radically different car to the Mark X/420G it ended up using virtually identical rear suspension to that car and the E Type (in fact the rear track width of the XJ was 4ft 10⅓in, within ⅓in of that of the 420G). It was also envisaged that the new car would utilise a 3-litre (2,997cc) engine developing around 185bhp, only 5bhp down on the 4.2-litre XK engine, but this engine did not produce sufficient low speed torque for a Jaguar saloon and was therefore abandoned in favour of a modified version of the existing 4.2-litre unit, backed up by a 2.8-litre alternative for tax-conscious European countries. Jaguar also experimented with a V8 unit after trials in a Mark X but due to major problems in obtaining sufficiently smooth running the idea was abandoned. It was also initially envisaged that the new XJ would use the now familiar 5.3-litre V12 engine, but as development work was not far enough advanced by the release date this option was also abandoned, if only temporarily.

Bodyshell

The bodyshell was to be as rigid as possible for passenger safety and secure handling, these being high priorities, so the torsional strength of the shell needed to be greater than on previous models. The bodyshells were produced as usual by Pressed Steel Fisher (although at a new location) and despite the greater rigidity of the XJ the new car was 840lb lighter than its predecessor. Of smaller dimensions than the previous model in most respects the new XJ also had a lower overall height than any other Jaguar saloon. The same principles of manufacture were employed as on the 420G by the use of many smaller panels welded together to form the whole.

The basis of the design was an immensely strong, heavily ribbed central platform forming the floor pan, with bracing provided by the sills and transmission tunnel. This assembly was further stiffened by means of two large box-section crossmembers, one under the front seats, the other just forward of the rear seat pan. With such inherent strength it became unnecessary to provide heavy screen pillars, thus giving the interior an airy, spacious feel.

At the front of the shell the two longitudinal members, inner wing panels and valances were welded up to form a strong fabricated assembly linked by a further structure surrounding the radiator incorporating an upper cross

ABOVE. Original styling drawings for the front of the XJ6, the right hand one being very close to the final concept.

Even in the mid sixties Jaguar still used full-size mock-ups to evaluate styling. This example, although still retaining adapted 420G bumpers and wheels, does show the XJ line and in particular the windscreen/side window areas taking shape.

Another styling mock-up in the Browns Lane car park shows the near complete XJ look, particularly in the frontal aspect, although still using adapted 420G indicator lenses.

Camouflaged XJ6 on rugged testing prior to public release.

Statutory impact test for the XJ6 at MIRA.

member, detachable to facilitate assembly. The bulkhead between the engine bay and passenger compartment was double skinned, and the ducting for the heating system formed a bracing between the front and rear bulkhead walls. The front wings were of the bolt-on type, which made them easily replaceable in case of damage or, in later life, for restoration. The design of the front shell assembly made for a very roomy engine bay, ideally suited to a wide range of engines including the yet to be announced V12.

At the rear the two box-section longitudinal members ran up and over behind the seat pan to meet the double-skinned boot floor; together with the boot, the inner wing panels and spare wheel well formed the tail assembly. The lower valance panels of the rear body sides behind the rear wheels were also bolted assemblies, thus providing easy access to the twin side-mounted 11½-gallon fuel tanks, which were enclosed within the shell but sealed off completely from the cabin and boot. (Twin AUF 303 electric fuel pumps were mounted underneath the boot floor).

The whole body structure, although very strong, still provided a "crushability" factor to comply with safety regulations — in fact over 18in of deformability was built into the XJ shell design. Bodyshells were treated to a 13-stage zinc-phosphate rustproofing procedure followed by dipping in a rust inhibiting paint for extra protection. After baking a primer coat was applied, then two primer-surface coats, and finally the main colour coats were applied and baked. The underside of the bodyshell was treated with a sealing compound. It is interesting to note that before the final top coats of paint were applied assembly and road-testing of vehicles took place. This was a tip picked up from other luxury car manufacturers to avoid blemishes and minor "man-made" flaws spoiling the final finish.

Comprehensive and effective sound deadening precautions were taken on all XJs, to the point that the box-section members to the rear of the door apertures were filled with padding to deaden road noise. Even the air ducts in the partitions in the front bulkhead were designed to cut down transference of noise from the engine bay.

As far as styling was concerned the new XJ was definitely in the Jaguar and William Lyons mould, bearing a surprising resemblance to the previous Mark X/420G shape. At the front the overall layout was the same as used on the 420G and 420 saloons, featuring exactly the same four separate headlights and chromium surrounds, with slim chromium-plated bumper and overriders, but with rectangular chromium-plated dummy horn grilles and extra large indicator/side light housings. All of these, apart from the headlights, were unique to the Series 1 XJ.

One of the pre-production XJ6s used for photographic purposes.

Rear view of one of the
very first XJ6s. Note the
straight exhaust tailpipes,
later re-shaped due to
passsenger complaints of
fumes. Note also the
simple winged
adornment either side of
the boot lock, the bumper
bar number plate
illumination and the total
lack of Jaguar badging.

BELOW. One of the very
first XJ6 4.2s with
manual/overdrive
transmission. Note the
front offside wing
mounting for the radio
aerial, standard practice on
early XJs.

Front view of the early
XJ6, simple, uncluttered,
without Jaguar badging
but unmistakably Jaguar in
style.

One of the most striking styling features of the new model was
undoubtedly the relatively simple and unadorned radiator grille, which
dispensed with heavy chromium surrounds. For the first time on any Jaguar
it had horizontal bars, crossed by five vertical bars, with a plastic badge at the
top. Again for the first time on any Jaguar the grille was wider than it was
tall, to suit the low-slung design of the whole car. A secondary grille was
featured below bumper level to aid cooling. Even more striking was the
absence of the familiar Jaguar mascot from the leading edge of the bonnet, a
move made necessary by changing legislation worldwide. Jaguar also felt it
unnecessary to adorn the bonnet with a chromium-plated centre strip as on
other Jaguars. The bonnet itself was a forward-hinged one-piece unit.

From the side the new XJ6 was very clean cut, with little unnecessary
adornment save for plastic leaping Jaguar badges sited at the bottoms of the
front wings, chromium plated window frames and rain gutters, and a single
coachline coinciding with the swage line of the body.

The track was quite wide: 4ft 10in at the front and 4ft 10$^{1}/_{3}$in at the rear;
this made the car look squat and purposeful when viewed from the front or
rear. The tyres, low profile ER70 VR 15, were of a new design, made by
Dunlop in conjunction with Jaguar specifically for the XJ saloons. With an
irregular tread pattern to prevent resonances, these tyres were a derivative
of the previous and successful SP Sport radials with aquajet drainage
system. They were fitted to 15in wheels with 6in rims, the widest fitted to
a Jaguar saloon up to that time. The standard steel wheels were always
finished in silver paint (gone were the days of body colour match) with
snap-fitting chromium-plated Rimbellishers and hub caps as used on the
420G, 420 and 240/340. Wire wheels were never available as a factory
option on the XJ due to concern about the tremendous cornering loads that

could be exerted, but chromium-plated steel wheels were later made available for certain models as an extra cost option.

From the rear the new XJ6 looked less traditionally Jaguar than any other part of the car, although the slim wrap-around bumper and overriders were clearly reminiscent of other Jaguar saloons of the sixties. The bumper itself was initially made in one piece (later three separate pieces with the overriders hiding the joins). The rear lighting treatment was new, with a cluster of indicator, brake and stop lights at the corners of the wings and separate reflectors and reversing lights on the boot lid flanking the number plate housing. This had a chromium-plated surround for the number plate and plain winged chromium-plated adornment either side of the boot lock. The rear number plate lamps were now situated in the bumper bar (a siting subsequently found to collect water, later modified). As the rear bumper was set quite high, a large valance (bolted on) was required below bumper level, with holes at either end to allow the chromium-plated exhaust pipes to protrude. There was a lockable chromium-plated fuel filler cap on top of each rear wing, replacing the previous model's flush fitting metal covers.

Badging on the first cars was kept to a minimum, with a simple "litre" identification badge (2.8 or 4.2) on the rear right hand side of the boot lid, or for the North American market an "XJ6" badge instead (the 2.8-litre car was not available in that market). On very early cars the scripted "Jaguar" was not featured, but later it was positioned to the left of the rear number plate. It was of the same style as used on all other Jaguars of the sixties.

For the US market XJ6s were supplied as standard with whitewall tyres and with side repeater lights on the front and rear wings.

Mechanics and Running Gear

Mechanically the XJ saloon was in many respects a development of previous Jaguar practice, with coil and wishbone type front suspension incorporating semi-trailing wishbones and an anti-roll bar, although the new suspension differed from previous types in two respects: anti-dive geometry and the use

Engine bay detail of the Series I XJ6 showing crossmember and steering column.

of outboard mounted dampers. Basically the front suspension was mounted as on the 420G except that the cross beam was a box-section member instead of a forged beam. This subframe was attached to the body via rubber mountings (made up of no less than six different compounds) and located longitudinally by large diameter rubber trunnions which had a carefully calculated compliance. The front engine mountings were fitted to the cross member, thus eliminating a good deal of engine vibration from the body structure.

Inclining the upper wishbone fulcrums upwards at 3½ degrees to the horizontal and the lower ones downwards at 4 degrees effectively altered the kingpin angle. This in effect reduced the tendency for the front springs to compress under load when the brakes were heavily applied. On braking the pressure on the wishbones tended to lift the car against the downward forces. A factor of 50% anti-dive geometry was chosen by Jaguar as being the ideal compromise, prividing "feel" to the car as a whole under braking. In line with this development Jaguar also fitted softer springs with a 25% reduction in spring rates and a total movement between bump and rebound of 7in. An anti-roll bar acting on the bottom wishbones was fitted, as on the previous models. Girling Monotube dampers containing pressurised gas/fluid to counteract temperature and frothing effects were employed, mounted outboard of the springs. These dampers provided extra travel, excellent anti-fade characteristics and much greater control. As the upper mountings of these new dampers were direct to the body, special top bushes of expanded polyurethene were devised for better noise insulation.

Rack and pinion steering was used on the XJ6 for the first time on any Jaguar saloon, with power assistance (standard on 2.8 de luxe and 4.2-litre

An underneath view of the engine compartment of a Series I XJ 6 clearly showing crossmember, steering rack and alloy sump.

cars, an extra cost option on 2.8-litre standard cars). The rack and pinion system was of an entirely new type developed with Jaguar by Adwest Engineering and Alford and Adler. The steering rack was mounted behind the suspension subframe for greater safety, with additional safety features built into the steering column. The upper column, made by AC Delco, consisted of two parts sleeved together and located by small plastic pins which would shear under heavy load, even the casing having a collapsible section. The lower column was connected by a universal joint, permitting the column to bend in a crash. There was also a swinging link at the bottom end to accommodate flexing of the cross member mountings. Metalastic mountings were employed to assist in absorbing road shocks. Adwest Varamatic power steering very similar to that used on the 420G was employed, pressure being supplied at 1,100 - 1,250psi from a vane type pump driven by a belt from the nose of the crankshaft, with spring-loaded jockey pulley to provide tensioning. The system worked well, with good "feel" (for its day) but with the minimum of required effort. Only 3.3 turns were needed from lock to lock.

Although Jaguar at one time considered an entirely new rear suspension system, they eventually chose the system employed on all independently sprung models since the introduction of the E Type in 1961, including the Mark X/420G and S Type and 420. This suspension has been well

documented in other publications, but essentially it was based on unequal length wishbones with fixed length driveshafts forming the upper wishbones. Heavy tubular transverse links with forged trunnions formed the bottom links and duplex spring and shock absorber units were fitted astride the driveshafts. Trailing radius arms were attached to the main structure with perforated type pancake rubbers. A Salisbury Hypoid bevel rear axle was used, with a 3.77:1 ratio on non-overdrive 4.2s (4.27:1 for 2.8s). Automatic transmission models had a 3.54:1 or 3.31:1 ratio for the 4.2-litre engine, or 4.27:1 on 2.8s, although these latter ratios were amended later in production for various overseas markets. A limited slip differential was not standard equipment on any version of the XJ6.

The whole of the rear suspension and axle assembly was mounted on a pressed steel subframe attached to the bodyshell behind the rear seat floor and suitably insulated against road noise and shock. The system has always been efficient, ensuring the road wheels are always kept in vertical contact with the road.

Jaguar remained loyal to Girling for the braking system on the XJ6, but the new system was far more sophisticated, based on all-round disc brakes with a dual-line braking system and tandem master cylinder. For the front brakes 11.87in discs were used, with ventilated shields and a three pot two pad system, having two smaller pistons on the outside of the disc and one larger piston on the inside. Although overall there was no increase in pad area this new arrangement did reduce brake fade considerably, at the same time increasing the life of brake pads. The caliper cylinder size at the front was 2.25in, and the brake pads were exactly the same as those used on the 420 and Series II E Type. At the rear 10.38in discs were fitted inboard as on all other independently sprung Jaguars, with a two pot caliper system, rear caliper cylinder size being $1^{11}/_{16}$in. A Girling tandem master cylinder with direct acting servo was employed, the brake pedal acting directly on to the master cylinder pushrods. The stop light switch also operated directly from the brake pedal.

The 4.2-litre (4,235cc) XK engine was basically the same power unit as used in the 420, with twin HD8 SU carburettors (or for the USA market twin Zenith-Stromberg 175CDs). The XK engine had first seen the light

The 4.2-litre XK engine adapted for the XJ6 with twin SU carburettors, alloy sump and, here, with the four-speed manual/overdrive gearbox.

of day back in 1948 in the XK120 sports car and even today, though no longer fitted to production Jaguars and Daimlers, is still used in certain vehicles for military use and in the Daimler DS 420 limousine. The engine was developed by Bill Heynes, Walter Hassan and Claude Baily during the war to power a new luxury postwar saloon which became the Mark VII. After various projects had been considered it emerged as a twin overhead camshaft six-cylinder unit with cast iron block, alloy head, and seven-bearing crankshaft. The camshafts were driven by separate top and bottom Reynolds duplex timing chains and actuated two valves per cylinder in hemispherical combustion chambers, the latter designed by Harry Weslake. The alloy pistons featured chromium-plated top rings with steel connecting rods lubricated by a gear pump driven from the front of the crankshaft. Initially of 3,442cc, the XK engine developed 160bhp at 5,000rpm with 195lb/ft of torque at 2,500rpm and a choice of 7:1, 8:1 or 9:1 compression ratios.

Not only had the designers built a very strong, powerful and smooth engine but they had made it aesthetically pleasing, with the aid of polished alloy camshaft covers, inlet manifold and carburettor dashpots, plus black vitreous enamelled exhaust manifolds. There is no doubt that the unit was well ahead of any competition at the time.

It was re-worked to give a capacity of 2,483cc for the mid-1950s 2.4-litre Mark I saloon, and then 3,781cc for use in the XK150 sports and Mark IX saloon, also finding a home in the Mark II, E Type and S Type. By this time a revised "B" type cylinder head had been developed and a new block with dry liners was used, the output increasing to 220bhp in twin carburettor form, while the E Type, XK150S and Mark X models had a triple carburettor version developing up to 265bhp at 5,500rpm.

A 4.2-litre version was introduced in 1964 on the E Type and Mark X. The extra capacity came from a bigger bore of 92.07mm, the cylinders being siamesed so that the same block size could be retained. The No. 1 and No. 6 cylinders were however moved outwards and the No. 3 and No. 4 cylinders were moved closer together. This change was accompanied by a new crankshaft with stronger bearings and a torsional damper. Other changes included a new inlet manifold, an alternator and a pre-engaged starter motor. The main purpose of the change to 4.2 litres was an increase in torque to 283lb/ft at 4,000rpm, while power output stayed the same but at lower revs — in fact the rev limit had been reduced. All 4.2-litre Series I XJ6s had a rotor arm rev limiter set to 5,400rpm.

At first the 4.2-litre unit looked like any other XK engine unit, with polished aluminium cam covers, but by the time the engine was fitted to the XJ saloons these had been replaced by black ribbed covers. Prior to the introduction of the XJ over 250,000 XK engines had been produced.

Very few changes had to be made to the unit to adapt it to the XJ, although XJ6 bonnets had a slight bulge to accommodate it — this being common to all XJs whatever engine was fitted. The XJ saw the first use of the long-stud engine. A larger oil filter was used, with a shuttle type oil pressure relief valve ensuring that all oil passing through the bearings was properly filtered. All models had a twin-pipe exhaust system with no less than four aluminised silencers to reduce noise and resonances.

Engine cooling was significantly improved on the XJ by means of a larger (3in) impeller on the water pump, a smaller pulley ensuring a faster turn rate at 1.25 times engine speed, a 1in larger water bypass hose (which on the 2.8 acted as the main water feed to the engine), water transfer holes in the cylinder head gasket (larger ones on the exhaust side to ensure a good flow of water around the ports) eliminating the need for a conventional water gallery on 4.2-litre engines, and a 12-bladed cooling fan with viscous coupling which automatically uncoupled at 2,500rpm. This latter item was claimed to save 75% on fan power requirement. A crossflow radiator system was used with separate header tank to keep the overall height down. On automatic transmission models a heat transfer pipe was fitted into the bottom hose.

Another variation on the XK engine theme was introduced with the XJ saloons, the 2.8-litre (2,791cc), the main reason being that such a small engine capacity fell below certain taxation thresholds in a number of European countries. Utilising the same straight port cylinder head and carburettors as the 4.2-litre, the 2.8 had a bore and stroke of 83 × 86mm, developing 180bhp at 6,000rpm, with 182lb/ft of torque at 3,750rpm.

Two types of transmission were available on the Series I XJ: manual four-speed (with or without overdrive) and automatic. The existing Jaguar four-speed all-synchromesh gearbox was employed, but with the helix angles of the constant mesh gears changed to 34 degrees, thus considerably reducing noise. An undercut taper on the selector dogs was employed to prevent gear jumping. A Laycock overdrive unit was available, operating on top gear only, and controlled by a gearlever mounted switch ideally situated for ease of operation. Incidentally, very few manual transmission cars were produced in the first year of production.

The automatic gearbox varied according to engine size, the 2.8-litre receiving the Borg Warner Model 35 unit whilst the 4.2-litre version was fitted with the Borg Warner Model 8. The Type 35 unit, for the first time on any Jaguar, featured two Drive positions, 1 and 2, giving greater flexibility of gear use in certain circumstances. Again for the first time on any Jaguar saloon the automatic transmission control was sited on the centre console where one would normally find the gear lever. The Model 8 unit on the larger engined cars was even then a bit long in the tooth but Jaguar had to wait for a new unit with sufficient strength to cope with the larger engines.

Interior fitments

It is fair to say that Jaguar put a great deal of thought and consideration into the design of the XJ6 interior, while at the same time retaining the traditional leather-and-walnut ambience so treasured by customers. The new car was a vast improvement on the 420G, with better seating, wider vision, and generally a greater degree of sophistication. The XJ6, although of smaller internal dimensions, allowed its occupants not only greater comforts but also improved ease of entry without the vast and heavy sloping doors and high sills of the previous model.

Starting with the seating, this was better proportioned, particularly for front seat passenger and driver, with greater lateral support and better shaping. These front seats were designed in part by the famous bed

Prototype XJ6 interior layout, almost right except for the strange steering wheel, minor finishing of switches, automatic transmission lever and switch identification legends.

Factory shot of Series I XJ6 De Luxe interior. A very traditional Jaguar layout with a confusing row of swithes in the centre panel. Note the simple wood finishers to the tops of the doors and the knurled knob to open and close the front quarterlight. On the centre console a blanking panel covers the radio fitting.

Manual/overdrive Series I XJ6, with overdrive switch conveniently sited on top of the gear lever. Note the bright aluminium trim on the radio/heater panel and console. This particular car was fitted with dictation equipment, but I doubt whether the centre console lid would close with the microphone connected!

manufacturers Slumberland (with "Posture" springing) and were over 10% lighter than conventional car seats. Both front seats were fully reclining, but on very early production models there was no provision for the fitting of head restraints. Seat facings were finished in traditional Connolly leather with aerated panels as on the 420G and 420, with side panels in Ambla. Disappointing for many long-time Jaguar owners was the absence of walnut picnic tables on the backs of the front seats, a move already made by other quality manufacturers such as Rolls-Royce to satisfy new North American legislation. The rear seat was of conventional design but again was better proportioned to hold the passengers firmly yet in comfort.

Prototype rear compartment of XJ6, with diagonal ribbing on the backs of the front seats, unfinished window winder and air grille in the rear parcel shelf.

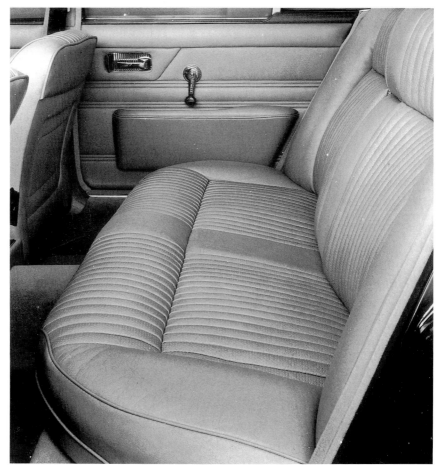

Production version of the rear compartment showing the final ribbing to the front seat backs and the seat belt fittings. Rear seat footroom was restricted: in this picture the front seats are set well forward.

Comparison between
Series I V12 and Series III
V12.

Series I XJs together:
Daimler Sovereign 4.2,
Jaguar XJ6 4.2 and Jaguar
XJ12 short wheelbase.

OPPOSITE. Series I XJ6
and V12 front views.
Note the plain vertical
grille bars of the V12.

XJ12 Series I swb saloon
in very period colour
scheme.

ABOVE. Daimler Double Six Vanden Plas Series I, top of the range.

Rear view of the Series I V12.

At this point mention should be made of the 2.8-litre Standard model, which was produced down to a price in order to capture fleet sales — a throw-back to the days of the Mark I saloon and the standard 2.4-litre model! The Standard model had no leather trim at all, seats being finished in Ambla and with no folding armrest in the rear seat. Simplified Ambla door panels were employed without the door pockets of the normal 2.8-and 4.2-litre cars. (Power steering, incidentally, was also not available on this basic 2.8-litre car.)

Referring back to the other models, good quality pile carpeting was employed, with thick underfelting to keep noise levels down, but even so complaints were received on the first production cars about excessive heat being transmitted through the floor from the exhaust system. A conventional nylon headlining was employed, as used on the 420 saloons.

New on a Jaguar were chromium-finished, flush-mounted door handles, in line with contemporary trends. Conventional window winding mechanisms and handles were used, although electric windows were available as an extra cost item, with individual switching from the centre console. Also new for Jaguar was the use of knurled knobs to control the front door quarterlights. Rear quarterlights were now permanently sealed. Banished along with the picnic tables were the traditional polished walnut door cappings, to be replaced by a very simple fillet of plain varnished wood.

As for the dashboard treatment, Jaguar had been careful not to go overboard, taking great pains to retain the established Jaguar "look", and this they did very well while at the same time bringing new printed-circuit technology into play. The basic layout was unchanged from the introduction of the Mark II saloon back in 1959, the two major instruments (speedometer and rev counter) with chrome bezels being positioned in front of the driver on a veneered panel. In between these was a very modern looking array of lights, banked together and providing indicator telltales, hazard warning lights, ignition light, brake warning light, and oil pressure warning light.

The equivalent panel on the passenger side hid the glove compartment, the inside of which was automatically lit upon opening. Its lid was fitted with a vanity mirror behind a spring-loaded panel. The centre veneered section held the four smaller instruments (oil pressure, fuel level, water temperature and battery condition indicator) along with clock, all mounted on a black ribbed plastic panel. The auxiliary switching was all new and of the rocker type (including light switches) but although the switches had a very positive action and looking very efficient they were ergonomically disastrous. As on previous Jaguar models the whole of the veneered centre dashboard section could be folded down for easy access to wiring and fuses. The ignition and starter switch had now been moved to the steering column (left of column on right hand drive vehicles) and was now a combined unit operated by the key (gone was the traditional Jaguar black starter button)!

The steering column, of the collapsible type with a two-spoke black steering wheel and half horn ring, could be adjusted for reach. Well positioned parcel shelves were to be found on either side of the dashboard area, giving limited but useful storage space for maps, cloths, etc. The centre console was "brightly finished" and perhaps a little out of character for a Jaguar, with aluminium alloy inlay panels for radio, heating/air conditioning controls (a feature first seen on the E Type 3.8 back in 1962 and correctly later abandoned on that model!) gearlever/quadrant, twin chromium-plated ashtrays, cigar lighter and rocker switches for electric window lifts where fitted. An excellent centre armrest finished off the centre console, with lift-up access to a flocked compartment for extra storage. Above the centre console a further flocked compartment was useful for parking tickets, pen storage, etc. At each end of the dashboard an "eye-ball" face level ventilator was fitted as part of the new and lavish heating/ventilation/air conditioning system of the XJ6.

Jaguar had for years had complaints from owners about inefficient heating systems. For the XJ6 a well established Smiths system was employed, drawing air through a windscreen mounted scuttle grille to a chamber where the air could be distributed heated or otherwise, and a complicated but nevertheless efficient system of valves was employed to direct the air to the interior of the car. The system could generate the equivalent of 5½kw, heating 160cfm of air to 82 degrees Centigrade and distributing it to any of five points: two at the top of the dashboard for demisting, two in the footwells in the front compartment, and one in the rear compartment via ducting to an eye-ball distribution point on the rear centre console (this last item eliminated on the Standard 2.8-litre model). Twin electric fans were employed to drive the air through the system, operated from a dash mounted rocker switch. Temperature selection was by means of a heat sensing tap with setting control on the centre console next to the radio. Opening and closing of flaps was by means of levers also positioned on the centre console. Cool air was fed from the incoming chamber to the face-level outlets on the dashboard.

The system devised by Jaguar to extract stale air from the interior (known as the Posivent Air Extractor System) involved a one-way outlet positioned in the centre of the rear parcel shelf. This outlet led to a low pressure area below the base of the rear window in a gap between the boot lid and rear bodywork.

A full Delaney-Gallay air conditioning system was an extra cost option available on 4.2-litre models only. The condenser unit was designed to fit into the existing heating system of the car without taking up valuable space elsewhere. Although this system was of benefit particularly for the North American market it was nowhere near as efficient as the home-based product found in contemporary Cadillacs and Lincolns, and while the heating and ventilation arrangements were a vast improvement on previous Jaguar models, it was clear even at this point that they still had some way to go to equal comparative product from manufacturers like Ford.

Boot

The XJ6 boot was well planned, with quite a low loading area and a distinct lack of internal obstructions, and offered something in the region of 17cu.ft of luggage space. The spare wheel was placed under the boot floor beneath a wooden lift-off panel. Gone, unfortunately, was the traditional Jaguar fitted tool box, replaced by a simplified set of hand tools in a black tool roll itself enclosed within a black holdall that contained the jack. Black Hardura floor matting was used, along with black-finished fibreboard panels lining the inner wings and the inside of the boot lid. Twin petrol tanks were mounted in the rear wings, initially of 11.5gals capacity each.

XJ6 prices on launch

2.8-litre Standard
Manual   £1,797
Manual with overdrive   £1,859
Automatic   £1,900

2.8-litre de luxe
Manual   £1,897
Manual with overdrive   £1,958
Automatic   £1,999

4.2-litre de luxe
Manual   £2,254
Manual with overdrive   £2,315
Automatic   £2,398

Extra cost options were
Seat Belts   £19
Electric windows   £59
Square foglamps, pair   £22
(for flush mounting in horn grilles)
Smiths Radiomobile   £48
Chromium plated wheels (set of 4)   £120
Air conditioning   £252
Laminated windscreen   £14

What the Press said

The first road impressions of the new Jaguar saloon came in September 1968 from *Autocar*, whose writer had been given the opportunity to try out the car a few weeks before the public launch. His first impressions — in relation to the superior ride and handling of the car and the uncanny lack of noise — were to be echoed by virtually all motoring journalists. *Car and Driver* in early 1969 recognised the XJ6 as one of the world's best balanced cars, offering traditional British quality with up-to-the-minute technology and styling.

One of the earliest road tests was published in March 1969 by *Car* magazine, who were quick to compare the new XJ to the other current

Pre-production XJ6 during splash testing at MIRA prior to public release.

Jaguar saloons, the 340, 420 and 420G. They realised the potential for the new car to replace all these on price, on performance and on equipment. They initially tested the top-of-the-range 4.2-litre XJ6, producing good acceleration figures of 0 to 60mph in 9.7 seconds and 0 to 100mph in 26.4 seconds. Even the fuel consumption was "acceptable" at a round figure of 16mpg. Again the handling was found to be excellent and controllable, with very responsive power steering.

From there on roadtesters in all the contemporary magazines gave glowing reports on the 4.2-litre saloon — *Motor* commenting "Jaguar sets impressive new standards; combination of performance, comfort, roadholding and quietness unrivalled at price with very few faults". In the *Autocar* test of the same year the unbelievable value for money and the car's superb adhesion were emphasised. The Australian *Modern Motor* magazine gave the new Jaguar the accolade of "Best British car of the decade — difficult-to-match standards". And so on. It was no wonder that journalists chose the XJ6 as the Car of the Year.

There were no published road tests of the 2.8-litre. Perhaps Jaguar felt, as they had with the 2.4-litre Mark II in the early sixties, that the model did not present the true Jaguar image of performance. Perhaps, in view of the many problems associated with the 2.8-litre engine, their decision was a wise one!

Competitors

As for the XJ6's rivals at the time, there was very little comparable on the British scene. Conceivably, the nearest home-grown equivalent in four-door luxury transport was the Rolls-Royce Silver Shadow or Bentley T Series. Sold at very substantially higher prices, the Crewe-built cars might be considered to be in a totally different ownership bracket, but in terms of handling, ride and performance they were no match for the Jaguar. To be fair to Rolls-Royce, however, their owners were not usually "sporting" and perhaps rated status and build quality above performance and handling. The only other British car that might have been seen as a rival was the Rover 3.5

in saloon or coupé form. A solidly built if rather traditional luxury car with a quality image, it was obviously not then or could ever really be in the Jaguar performance bracket. Although very comfortable, with a reasonably good ride, this car's antiquated chassis did nothing for its handling and it was overdue for replacement.

On the European stage the Jaguar competed then as now with Mercedes-Benz and BMW. M-B's 280SE was much more expensive than the Jaguar and slower in top speed (although an equal performer on acceleration), while the 2.8-litre engine was never that sophisticated or refined. Fuel consumption was however better than the Jaguar's, but the level of trim was, as now, always a step behind the British car's. The BMW in the shape of the relatively new 2800 series had soon gained a good following in England, but it wasn't as quick as the Jaguar, as refined, or as well equipped.

In the North American market the Jaguar was on its own. Although the Cadillacs, Chevrolets and Buicks were cheaper, the Jaguar had better overall performance, more refinement, leather-and-walnut trim and, perhaps most important, the British quality image.

How the early cars fared

Even after 12 months of production XJs were still hard to come by, with premium prices being asked for used examples. Some of the magazines had been given the use of XJ6 4.2-litre saloons on long-term assessment, and their reports made interesting reading. Interestingly, in one such test performance and fuel consumption remained very close to the original road test figures (the long-term assessment car being an automatic transmission version). Within the first 8,000 miles the only faults recorded amounted to a faulty alternator and passenger complaints of petrol fumes in the rear compartment. Apart from routine maintenance and minor faults caused by the garages rather than by the car itself, the car behaved perfectly during the rest of the first twelve months, the magazine reporting only that the rear window trim came adrift and that the front doors had dropped slightly.

An American survey of XJ owners was carried out in 1971, 247 being canvassed with an amazingly high response of 107. Of these, 39 had had no problems at all with their cars and 84 actually thought the XJ saloon was the best car they had ever owned! Asked what other cars they had considered before picking the Jaguar, 60 had given consideration to Mercedes, 21 to Cadillac, 14 to Lincoln, 7 to BMW, 4 to Rolls-Royce and 1 to American Ford. Loyalty to previous marques did not appear to have made any difference, although 28 from the survey had previously owned Jaguars.

Some complaints were received about performance, which was obviously not up to E Type or 3.8-litre Mark II standards, but the majority reported the best characteristics as being comfort and handling. Surprisingly, as XJs were still relatively rare in America at this time, most surveyed did not consider the Jaguar unique or imposingly different. Over half those surveyed had experienced faults with their Jaguars, the majority being miscellaneous minor problems including ill-fitting trim panels and wind noise. The commonest

Browns Lane assembly plant, with Series I saloons coming off the line.

faults concerned the electrics, with one particular car's electrical system failing entirely. Next most commonly reported faults concerned the air conditioning, which didn't match up to the standards of North American cars. Most owners considered dealer service relatively good without being excellent. On overall percentage ratings the XJ6 gained over 92% on brakes, cornering, instrumentation, boot area, and steering, with the highest marks of 96% going to ride and comfort. The car still recorded over 85% on other items such as visibility, room, quietness, performance and finish.

As already mentioned, no road tests were carried out on the 2.8-litre XJ6, but one owner's report did appear in *Competition Car* in 1972, based on a manual/overdrive model. Although admittedly underpowered when compared to the 4.2-litre version, the 2.8-litre was found to cruise comfortably at 110mph with four people up, and normal conversation with windows up could be maintained easily at 100mph. With only 6,000 miles on the clock no report was made of piston problems, experienced later by many owners.

Out of 71 vehicles entered for the coveted Car of the Year award in 1969 the testers and analysts recognised the qualities that set the XJ6 apart from the others. In L.J.K. Setright's own words, "Indeed, to my mind the Jaguar is not merely remarkable for what it is, but also because it makes redundant all cars that cost more. I can think of no car of which this can be as truthfully said, and I would consider this fact alone as qualifying the XJ6 for your award". Reviewing subsequent Cars of the Year and road tests of other luxury saloons it emerges that no other vehicle received so much praise until the 1986 launch of the "new" XJ6, the XJ40.

Series 1: Expansion and Improvement

The new car was much in demand and even after eighteen months of production some customers were still awaiting delivery. As usual with any new model, a continual process of improvement must take place, both planned and otherwise, to deal with faults identified and changes in fashion and technology. Jaguar needed to do this and to expand the model range to suit a wider range of customers, while maintaining the basic concept with interchangeability of parts to keep costs down.

With market expansion in mind Jaguar had always planned that a Daimler derivative would be made available and that a re-engined version would be offered, of either V8 or V12 configuration. The model range would ultimately expand further with the availability of two wheelbase lengths as well as two-door options.

The new Daimler Sovereign

As has already been mentioned the Daimler 420 Sovereign soldiered on in production alongside the new Jaguar XJ6. It did so until August 1969, when production finally ceased without any apparent immediate replacement. Then, two months later on 9th October 1969, the all-new Daimler Sovereign, based on the XJ6, was announced. Although the Jaguar-based DS 420 limousine was still available to order, the V8 250 saloon had also been discontinued, which meant that Jaguar had reduced the Daimler range to virtually one car. Not only this, but the new Daimler Sovereign was entirely Jaguar mechanically, with no reprieve for the well-balanced V8 engines designed by the old Daimler company.

The new Sovereign was therefore very much a badge engineered version of the XJ6, available in both 2.8- and 4.2-litre versions (although not as a 2.8-litre standard model). The only differences externally amounted to a well proportioned (and perhaps better looking) fluted radiator in the Daimler tradition, a fluted plinth on the boot to match, Daimler badging and hub caps, and a chromium-plated strip down the centre of the bonnet. Daimler variants had the same range of colour schemes as Jaguar models. Mechanically there were no changes, save for the fact that overdrive on manual transmission models was standard equipment — but few manual

ABOVE. Daimler
Sovereign Series I with
traditional fluted grille.

Rear view of the Daimler
Sovereign Series I (in this
case a 2.8-litre version).
Note the ribbed boot lock
surround, the Sovereign
badging and the straight
tailpipes of the early cars.

Daimler Series 1s were actually produced. Daimler badging was also added to the engine camshaft covers. Internally, there was new badging on the steering wheel boss and centre console, along with redesigned door panels with wider armrests and pulls in the front, and a black vinyl covering on the upper section of the door panels with a bright chromium-plated horizontal strip. The seating, although of exactly the same style as on the Jaguar versions, did (and still does to this day) have wider pleats (seven in number), without the aerated panels.

A novel extra-cost option listed on early Daimlers was a radio/cassette system with stereo output and microphone for dictation purposes.

The launch prices of the Daimler Sovereigns were:

2.8-litre manual/overdrive	£2,356
2.8-litre automatic transmission	£2,417
4.2-litre manual/overdrive	£2,713
4.2-litre automatic transmission	£2,805

The Daimler versions proved very popular in England as many owners admitted to preferring the shapely Daimler radiator grille to the rather undistinguished Jaguar style. In two successive years a Daimler 4.2-litre Sovereign won a Gold Medal for Bodywork in the "no price limit" section at the Motor Show.

Enter the V12 "A special kind of motoring which no other car in the world can offer"

Although a phrase long associated with Jaguar, this had particular relevance when the long awaited XJ12 was launched to the public on 11th July 1972. It had been delayed several times over the previous two years through

Jaguar XJ12 Series I in original short wheelbase form, distinguished by its vertical grille bars and V12 badge.

ABOVE. Although the XJ bodyshell was designed to accommodate a V12 (or V8) power unit, with the V12 engine installed there is little room left. Note particularly the battery box with its own cooling fan and the absence of the air conditioning pump and piping that further clutters the later cars. This is an early Series I V12 engine with four Zenith Stromberg carburettors.

development problems, and then released at a time of labour unrest at Browns Lane which eventually led to a strike. The XJ bodyshell had been designed to take a larger engine, and Jaguar decided upon the installation of the V12 unit as used in the E Type Series III. The XJ12, with development costs of around £3 million, gave Jaguar a commanding position, particularly in the North American market. Whilst a V8-powered XJ would have been nice, Jaguar were not happy about the inherent vibration problems, so a V12 seemed the ideal configuration, providing also the bonus of prestige. The Jaguar XJ12 became the only mass-produced V12-engined saloon available in the world, upstaging in America the V8s seen in everything from Ford Fairlane to Cadillac stretch limos. It also put Jaguar in the record books, for the new model was voted Car of the Year in 1973 and was the fastest production saloon car in the world for some considerable time, a title previously held by Jaguar with the 3.8-litre Mark II many years earlier.

The V12 engine was created by the same team as the XK six-cylinder unit: Walter Hassan, Claude Baily and Bill Heynes, with help from Harry Mundy. Of 5,343cc, it developed 265bhp at 6,000rpm (155bhp per ton) and 301lb/ft of torque at 3,500rpm. Developed from the four-cam V12 racing engine originally planned for the XJ13 racing/prototype, the production engine featured only one overhead camshaft for each bank of cylinders, to save cost and weight. With bore and stroke measurements of 70mm × 90mm the V12 unit had alloy block and heads, a seven main bearing cast crankshaft of EN16T steel, chain driven camshafts and a compression ratio of 10.6:1 (later amended to 9:1). Carburation was by way of four Zenith/Stromberg 175CD emission-controlled carburettors fed by air ducted from slim, shaped AC filter units following the shape of the bonnet. Jaguar may well have considered using the traditional SU carburettors had it not been for the restricted height under the bonnet of the XJ. The Strombergs were placed outside the 60 degree vee. A beautifully engineered throttle capstan was developed for smoothness of operation.

A specially produced ignition system by Lucas (called "Oscillating Pick-up System") with solid state circuitry was used, along with a new crossflow radiator divided into two sections for better temperature control. The radiator contained no less than four gallons of coolant, its heat controlled by a four bladed Airscrew electric fan with Bosch motor plus a conventional 17in steel engine fan with Torquattrol viscous coupling. An oil cooler was fitted to the bottom of the radiator.

Measures had to be taken in other areas to deal with the vast amount of heat developed by the V12 engine in such a confined engine bay. A recirculating fuel system had to be devised to prevent evaporation of fuel in the under-bonnet area, stainless steel heat shields were fitted around the steering rack and engine mountings, and heat shielding was also provided along the full length of the underbody to protect the shell from the heat generated by the exhaust system. Even the battery (under the bonnet near the bulkhead) received special attention, receiving a steel casing containing a thermostatically controlled electric fan activated at temperatures above 55 degrees Centigrade.

This magnificent engine, initially tested in the old Mark X and launched in 1971 in the E Type, was a true triumph of engineering and weighed in at only 680lb (only 80lb heavier than the old XK six-cylinder unit) through the extensive use of alloys. Dimensionally the unit was large, at 39in long, 27in high and 39in wide. This altered weight distribution in the car, with 53.8% at the front (compared with 52.8% in the XJ6) and 46.2% at the rear (47.2% in the XJ6). To combat the extra weight over the front wheels, uprated and lengthened front springs were employed: 680lb/308kg compared with 600lb/272kg on the six-cylinder models. (They were uprated still further on air conditioned models, which were even heavier.) Stronger front wishbones were also employed but no other changes took place in the suspension..

Changes were, however, needed to cope with the increased performance of the V12 car. Ventilated front disc brakes were employed for the first time, of 11.18in diameter and .94in thickness, as used on the E Type. A Kelsey-Hayes brake balance valve was fitted to guard against rear wheel lock-up under heavy braking, and a Girling Supervac brake servo with additional reserve polypropylene tank fitted under the right hand front wing was used. The rear brakes remained unchanged.

Tyres and wheels also needed to be uprated so Dunlop developed a new version of their special XJ6 tyre, E 70 VR15, with a nylon casing and steel breaker strip to cope with the car's extra weight. Although new steel wheels with extra ventilation slots were used 6in rims remained the norm for all XJ saloons.

The XJ12 had a matt black finish on the radio and heating control panel, and on the centre console.

This particular V12 (also applicable to XJ6s) was fitted with the optional electric window lifts, operated by resited 420G-style switches on the centre console armrest.

Revised door trim panels for the Series I V12 with longer armrests (the speaker grilles were not standard).

The exhaust system on the V12 cars was virtually unchanged from the six-cylinder versions save for the heat shields already mentioned and a small increase in the bore of the pipes from 1⅞in to 2in. For the rear end a Salisbury Power-Lok differential was standard equipment, with a ratio of 3.31:1 producing 22.9mph per 1,000rpm in top gear. The new XJ12 was only available with an automatic gearbox due to the preference for this type of transmission in North America. A Borg Warner Model 12 unit was fitted, as on later versions of the XJ6. Ironically, the V12 models, despite heavier fuel consumption, still used the standard 23-gallon fuel tanks!

Externally there was little difference between the six- and twelve-cylinder cars. Revised badging displaying at the rear the XJ12 emblem was used along with a gold on black V12 badge at the centre of the radiator grille. The grille itself was entirely new, with vertical slats only, giving a more pleasing look than the "egg-crate" grille used on the six-cylinder cars.

Internally, minor changes were made including the fitment of Daimler Sovereign type door panels, black PVC trim covering for the centre console and radio panel area (replacing the garish aluminium finish of the XJ6), a gold V12 badge on the centre console and a manual choke control situated under the dash panel. A 7,000rpm rev counter was fitted along with a 160mph speedometer.

The XJ12 was introduced at a price of £3,725, amazing value for money for such a sophisticated, complex and fast saloon. This price was for the base car, such items as air conditioning being at this time still extra-cost options even on V12s.

The Daimler Double Six and Double Six Vanden Plas

A Daimler version of the V12-engined Jaguar was announced one month after the XJ in August. It was called the Daimler Double Six, reviving an old Daimler name. Apart from the usual fluted treatment to front and rear ends, badging and the black finished trim at the top of each door panel, the Double Six was totally Jaguar. It wore exactly the same grille as the six-cylinder Daimler. Yet more was in store for the Series 1 XJ: on 26th September 1972 the most prestigious model yet, the Daimler Double Six Vanden Plas saloon, was announced, relaunching another well-known and respected name. To quote Jaguar/Daimler advertising of the period, "All Daimlers are exclusive, aristocratic, distinctive, their levels of luxury and refinement are unsurpassed. Yet even the traditional Daimler standards are excelled in the latest Vanden Plas models".

Effectively this was a standard Daimler Double Six saloon with a modified bodyshell giving 4in of extra length in the rear passenger and door area to provide better legroom, yet without affecting the overall balance and look of the superb styling. Before painting the Vanden Plas models were sent down to the Vanden Plas coachworks in Kingsbury, London for final finishing to a very high standard. This included a matching or contrasting colour vinyl roof, extra and better paint finishes, better quality Connolly seats and

The most prestigious Series I was the Daimler Vanden Plas model, with 4in longer wheelbase and extra external adornment including twin spotlamps, chrome waist trim, chromium-plated wheels and vinyl roof.

trim containing an extra 10% of leather. And there was more, including specially made and separately contoured front and rear seats (à la Mark IX saloon), better quality veneer on the dashboard and door fillets (both with whitewood inlays), door mirrors as standard equipment, waist chrome trim, chromium-plated wheels, and of course special badging at the rear. Extra sound deadening padding, higher quality carpeting with nylon over-rugs, rear compartment reading lamps and a radio/cartridge player were also part of the package.

The Vanden Plas models had their own very distinctive range of exterior colour schemes:

Aegean Blue
Aubergine
Caramel
Coral
Morello Cherry
Sage
Silver Sand

At a launch price of £5,363 the Daimler Double Six Vanden Plas was significantly costlier than any other Jaguar/Daimler model, but it was nonetheless very competitive when compared with Rolls-Royce, Bentley or even the best of Mercedes.

Long-wheelbase models

One month later in October 1972 came the launch of another phase of the XJ Series 1 saloons, the long-wheelbase models, added to the standard range and known as XJ6L and XJ12L in both Jaguar and Daimler Sovereign forms. This development, first seen on the Vanden Plas, was prompted by

Mercedes-Benz's introduction of a long wheelbase "S" class saloon. Basically the only change to the normal cars was an extra 4in of body length (in the floorpan and rear doors) to provide extra comfort for rear seat passengers. It added 1.5cwt to the weight of the car but this had little effect on performance. The existing short-wheelbase models remained in production alongside the new models.

Long-wheelbase saloons had an extra 4in of wheelbase to provide more leg room for rear seat passengers, necessitating longer rear doors.

Rear compartment of the long-wheelbase saloon showing the extra legroom.

Modifications

Apart from model changes and introductions there had been many detail modifications to the cars since their initial launch. Early in 1969, after continuous complaints from owners about exhaust fumes reaching the interior whenever windows were left open, Jaguar realised that the shape of the exhaust tailpipes was causing the problem. They were straight, and gases were getting caught up in the airflow of the car and being pulled back along the side of the bodywork to the passenger area. By giving a distinct curvature to the rear pipes, this problem was eliminated.

Due to some confusion among dealers and customers Jaguar were forced to submit a service bulletin in February of 1969 warning that the Type 35 Borg Warner automatic transmission fitted to the 2.8-litre models did not have a rear pump, making towing the car a dangerous operation which could cause serious damage through non-lubrication of the internal parts of the gearbox. They therefore recommended towing with the rear wheels off the ground or with the propshaft disconnected. Further confusion also arose in connection with adjusting the rear brake bands on the automatic transmission of both 4.2 and 2.8 models; due to the wording in the original Service Manuals it was easy for a mechanic to mis-read the figures for the two totally different transmissions and therefore adjust incorrectly.

Jaguar seemed to acknowledge a lot of initial problems with transmissions when in October 1969 they had to ask dealers to ensure that adjustments of the lock control linkage or switch were being made correctly — over 75% of all inhibitor switches returned to them by dealers as faulty were found to be in perfect working order!

Exhaust pipe rattles and leaks were complained of by some owners, particularly on automatic transmission 4.2-litre models, and this was found to stem from difficulties in removing the transmission oil pan, which was fouled by the exhaust pipes. Some mechanics were levering the pipes away, causing them to loosen and leak, instead of disconnecting the exhaust manifold to move the pipes to get at the oil pan.

Early cars were not fitted with head restraints but by August 1969 these became available on the front seats as an extra-cost option; normally, black (or seat-coloured) grommets filled the holes. By this time it was also possible to specify inertia reel seat belts as opposed to the untidy "loose" type, although again at extra cost. In 1970, too, footwell fresh air ventilators were fitted, fed from grille inlets in the dipped beam headlamp surrounds. Improved door locking was also fitted at this time. In May of the same year a new interior mirror arrived and non-reflective instrument bezels, switch and ventilator surrounds replaced the chromium-plated type previously used. To improve the provision for radio/cassette systems Jaguar made available extra fittings for the door panels to allow for four-speaker installations.

Externally the cars altered little during the period of Series 1 production. In August 1969 mud flaps became available as a factory-fitted extra-cost option and in October 1970 the front wheelarch flanges were altered in shape to give extra clearance between tyre and the wing. Before the end of 1970 the front windscreen's plated surround was altered and made much slimmer in appearance. In March 1971 the rear bumper was redesigned as three separate sections, the two wrap-around side members meeting the centre section under the over-riders to avoid an unsightly join. This reduced replacement costs if damage occurred and also facilitated fitting. For a short period an extra exterior colour option, Almond, was available, commonly seen on 2.8-litre versions of the XJ6.

Mechanically the Series I cars were amended in many more ways. The 2.8-litre engine had been a source of concern and embarrassment to Jaguar since its release to the public. From the start, complaints came from owners and distributors about unreliability and, in particular, holed pistons. At first

SERIES I DAIMLER AND V12

Jaguar could find no reason for these piston failures but after further testing and inspection of faulty units it became clear that a build-up of deposits was taking place in the combustion chambers and on the piston crowns. These caused premature detonation, eventually burning holes through the pistons. The problem was compounded by the fact that the exhaust valves were too close to the pistons.

Nothing of this kind had come to light during Jaguar's exhaustive testing of prototypes as they had been driven hard and fast, thus avoiding a build-up of carbon. In everyday use on the road, however, it was easy to build up such deposits, the inescapable conclusion being that if 2.8-litre owners had consistently thrashed their cars from the start things may not have turned out so badly for Jaguar (or the luckless owners).

In March 1970 Jaguar recommended that exhaust valve clearance should be increased to .008in from .006in, and in April specified the fitting of Champion N7Y spark plugs to replace the N9Y. In June the factory started to fit uprated pistons as standard (from engine no. 7G.8849) and made them available for earlier engines, but to little effect. In April 1971 an improved crankshaft rear oil seal was fitted to 2.8-litre engines.

As previously stated, the 2.8-litre car was never very popular and the Standard model least popular of all. This version was dropped from the range in March 1972 and the last 2.8-litre car for the home market was completed in May 1973, the last delivery to a dealership being in July. The 2.8-litre did, however, soldier on for various key European markets until the introduction of the Series II models.

In January 1969 all 4.2-litre versions except those destined for the USA and Canada received a revised rear axle ratio of 3.31:1 instead of 3.54:1 with, of course, revised speedometer to match. At the same time 2.8-litre cars (except USA and Canada) also got a revised axle ratio: 4.09:1 replacing 4.27:1. These gave higher top speeds with reduced engine revs. In April 4.2 automatic models for most European countries received a 3.07:1 axle ratio instead of 3.31:1 and cars for Austria and Switzerland also had a Powr-Lok differential standardised.

In March 1969 on XJs with manual transmission the oil filler plug was moved to a higher position on the right hand side of the gearbox, increasing oil capacity by ½pt to 4½pt. In November the top gear selector forks were altered to prevent 3rd to 4th gear crashing taking place. The same month, starting at engine no. 7L.1630, 4.2s received an improved type of clutch unit incorporating a higher rated diaphragm spring to prevent clutch slip at high mileage. In May the 4.2 model received stiffer front springs, from chassis nos. 1L.2671 (rhd) and 1L.51097 (lhd).

All early Series I cars suffered badly from petrol fumes in the cabin (particularly for rear seat passengers) and this was effectively cured by the fitting of new petrol filler caps with an anti-surge flap. A revised handbrake linkage was used with improved clevis pin for longer life. In November 1969 special heat shields were fitted between the body and exhaust to reduce heat transference to the front passenger compartment. Modified exhaust downpipes were also fitted to allow greater clearance between the pipes and the Borg Warner automatic transmission dipstick (the dipstick itself was also

41

modified in shape). An improved bonnet catch mounting proved necessary for better rigidity. By March 1970 emission-type exhaust manifolds were standardised for all models. In the same month the original XK type camshaft sprocket adjuster plate with vernier replaced the new XJ type with lobes which had caused problems and could result in damage to valve gear. Retrospectively all cars were subsequently altered on instructions from the Jaguar Service Department at Browns Lane to dealerships.

In October 1969 it was noted that the flared metal intake on the air cleaner of 2.8s could produce depressions in the air cleaner. A new cleaner (C.31073/1) featured a Neoprene flared intake instead. In the same month a modified inlet manifold (C.31975) was fitted to 2.8s, shortened at the front to provide improved access for distributor contact breaker adjustment. In November new camshafts giving quieter valve operation were fitted to engines from 7G.5795 (2.8) and 7L.8344 (4.2), identified by the addition of a groove machined in the periphery of the end flange. At around the end of 1969, at chassis numbers 1L.4988 rhd and 1L.57295 lhd, a most significant change took place with the adoption of the Borg Warner Model 12 automatic transmission, replacing the old-fashioned and "notchy" Model 8 on 4.2 models. The new 'box gave smoother gear changes, better acceleration at 0-60mph in 8.8 seconds as opposed to 10 seconds, and was generally a much stronger unit. A new and better gear selection range was used on the Model 12: instead of the usual P (park), R (reverse), N (neutral), D (drive), L (low) selection, the new transmission offered a P, R, N, D, 2, 1 arrangement with no "barrier" between selection of positions 2 and 1. The D position gave normal Drive mode with all three gears being used according to throttle opening. Selection of "2" gave intermediate gear only with no upshifts or downshifts possible, and "1" replaced the old L position, holding first gear only, again with no upshifts or downshifts. The selector positions caused some confusion for years as the 4.2-litre handbook implied that there was a "stop" between the positions "2" and "1", which there wasn't!

The old throttle-cable kickdown system of the previous transmission was replaced by an electro microswitch for full kick-down and a vacuum control system for part-throttle changes consisting of a pipe conveying

Later Series I saloons featured ventilated outer headlamp surrounds.

engine manifold depression to a vacuum servo mounted at the rear of the transmission. Hydraulic line pressures were therefore partly controlled by manifold depression, with smoothness of gearchanges being adjusted by means of an adjuster screw located in the servo unit. The original vacuum unit was changed in April 1971 for a much smaller version with a shorter pushrod to the throttle valve.

The new transmission gave much better driver control without the need to use the throttle opening to change gears at selected moments. This new gearbox was also better suited to the torque of the 4.2-litre engine and the forthcoming V12 unit. The 2.8-litre cars continued to use the Model 35 automatic transmission throughout its production.

In January 1970 (and of particular interest to those purely concerned with originality!) Jaguar fitted revised cylinder head cam covers incorporating drilled and tapped mounting holes for exhaust emission air ducts at engine nos. 7G.6125 (2.8) and 7L.8474 (4.2). In March the factory had to alter the shape of the bottom water hose (radiator to bottom pipe) due to rubbing through caused by the fan belt when on full adjustment. In the same month the upper radiator fan cowl of the air conditioned cars was standardised on all 4.2-litre models, with changes to water hoses at the same time. Also in that month, due to constant complaints of fuel starvation, Jaguar recommended all dealers to clean out the fuel line filters every 6,000 miles instead of 12,000.

April saw the fitting of a revised spare wheel cover and fuel pump cover in the boot, which meant resiting the jack and tool roll to the upper boot by means of a retaining bracket. In the same month the scuttle ventilator grille was changed to a satin chrome finish to avoid glare in the windscreen, from chassis nos. IG.5272 (2.8 rhd), IG.52459 (2.8 lhd), IL.7452 (4.2 rhd) and IL.53778 (4.2 lhd).

In June laminated windscreens became standard equipment for many European markets (due to changes in legislation) and a wider choice of windscreens became available on all cars, including:

Clear toughened (standard)
Sundym toughened
Clear laminated
Sundym laminated
Sundym laminated with shaded tint area to top

In July 1970 a revised brake fluid reservoir was adopted, positioned on the inboard side of the booster, instead of at the rear. In March 1971 SU HS8 carburettors were standardised, with a revised automatic enriching device for cold starting. A small guard was fitted over the fan on the front of the alternator as a safety measure. Due to complaints of noise transmitting from the speedometer cable to the interior of the car, a polythene sleeve was fitted over the cable, which was also re-routed to cure the problem.

In October of that year, by which time Jaguar had received many complaints of front tyres fouling the wheel-arches under severe cornering, a directive was issued to service departments to cut back the flange on the metal wheel-arch by approximately 6mm on existing cars, if necessary. Also in October a cosmetic change took place with the supply on all new cars from chassis nos. IG.6820 (2.8 rhd), IG.55465 (2.8 lhd), IL.10195 (4.2 rhd) and IL.55487 (4.2 lhd) of new door tread plates incorporating the name "Jaguar". At the same time a revised water temperature gauge and sensor were fitted on all XJs, with easier-to-read calibrations. This change coincided with the new finish on the previously chrome bezels, now matt black on all instruments. Later, in January 1972, a new oil pressure gauge calibrated to 100psi instead of 60psi was introduced.

In December 1970 the fuel line filter was relocated in the spare wheel compartment (previously sited there only on air conditioned models). Later it was fitted with a guard to protect against accidental damage. Also in December engine numbers were modified, letters being used to replace the former figures to identify compression ratios: "H" denoting high compression, "S" standard and "L" denoting low. A new "hot line" heated rear screen of toughened instead of laminated glass was fitted to all XJs, easily identifiable by the horizontal wires of the heated element.

By the end of 1970 weekly production of XJs at Browns Lane had increased to 650.

In January 1971, due to structural alterations in the front wings of all XJs, it became no longer possible to fit radio aerials on them. All future aerial installations were to be on the rear wings although a few owners did opt for the more expensive roof-mounted position.

In March 1971 the revised rear bumper bar assembly mentioned earlier was made available as a replacement when damaged or as new equipment on all subsequent XJs from chassis nos. IG.8194 (2.8 rhd), IG.54708 (2.8 lhd), Il.13172 (4.2 rhd) and IL.58287 (4.2 lhd). It was made up of three individual pieces bolted together behind the overriders. These overriders and the brackets remained unchanged.

In December 1971 diecast-bodied oil pumps were fitted to all engines at nos. 7G.16343 (2.8) and 7L.31456 (4.2).

From March of 1972 all non-air conditioned models received a 13psi radiator filler cap (replacing the 4psi type).

In June of that year chassis numbers were relocated from the left wing valance to the right wing valance.

In July, to prevent oil surge in extreme circumstances, Jaguar supplied a neoprene collar insert for existing XJ12 engines to fit over the oil dipstick. This effectively altered the oil capacity of the engine to 19 pints. A new type of dipstick was fitted to subsequent models.

By February of 1974 V12s had received a new "high load" coil and amplifier to improve spark plug performance, commencing at engine no. 7P.8169.

Many other changes took place during the production period of the XJ Series I, of which a small selection follows. A "stop" was incorporated in the front seat reclining mechanism to prevent the seat returning to an over-upright position when released. Due to complaints from very hot countries a revised rear parcel shelf of much stiffer material was used to prevent warping in extreme heat. Flies and other foreign bodies accumulated under the scuttle ventilator over a period of time, so Jaguar fitted a mesh

under the grille to prevent such objects getting into the heating system. To coincide with EEC regulations the reversing lights were enlarged, with new reflectors fitted below the rear light clusters. The front side/indicator lights were also slightly altered to accommodate new regulations. Due to complaints of oil leaks from the sumps on 4.2 litre cars, an improved oil sump gasket was fitted.

In September of 1973 Jaguar decided to cease production of the short wheelbase XJ12 and Daimler Double Six although the six-cylinder variants still remained available in both wheelbases.

The cars were still excellent value for money when compared with many foreign imports but prices had steadily increased during the production run. An example of the escalating price of a manual/overdrive model XJ6 through the years is given below.

Later Daimler Series I showing the larger reversing lights, repositioned reflectors, resited radio aerial and altered tailpipe shape. Jaguar models received the same treatment.

October 1968	£2,315
October 1969	£2,537
October 1970	£2,690
October 1971	£2,910
October 1972	£3,138

An interesting note concerns the supply of lock keys for the XJ. Although no mention was ever made of the matter in handbooks, manuals and the like, as well as the two sets of keys supplied with all cars, a further extra ignition key was always secured by a screw to the radiator top rail on the left hand side under the bonnet.

Colour schemes

Colour schemes available for Series I XJ as standard equipment in low bake or air dry form were:

Colours	Low Bake Ref.	Air Dry Ref.
Black	LSC.5030	GL.5030
Sable	LSC.25734	GL.25734
Ascot	LSC.26896	GL.26896
Regency Red	LSC.27420	GL.27420
British Racing Green (to Oct. '70 only	LSC.24400	GL.24400
British Racing Green (1970 on)	LSC.28461	L.28461
Special Police White	LSC.24048	GL.24048
Willow Green	404-2017	404-1888
Signal Red	504-0020	416-0021
Cream (to Oct. '70 only)	0765X0010	0765X0015
Old English White (replacing above)	3765X0010	765X0011
Warwick Grey	0765F2613	6170X6380
Light Blue	M072-4385	M070-4385
Pale Primrose	M087-6974	M070-6074
Dark Blue	M072-4647	M070-4647
Light Silver	M079-3308	P031-3308

By 1972/73 the following colours had been added to the above range:

Heather	LSC.29499	GL.29499
Turquoise	LSC.29136	GL.29136
Lavender Blue (replacing Light Blue)	LSC.29500	GL.29500
Green Sand (replacing Willow)	LSC.23055	GL.23055
Fern Grey	LSC.29047	GL.29047

All the above colours were available for XJ6s, V12s and Daimlers. Almond was also added for a limited period. Jaguar themselves only supplied air dried paint in appropriate gallon, pint or quart cans, or as touch-up. Low bake paint had to be specially requested from Jaguar's paint manufacturers.

Production figures

After five years of production no less than 98,129 Series I models in various forms had been made, based on the following:

Jaguar six-cylinder	78,891
Daimler six-cylinder	15,139
Jaguar V12	3,220
Daimler V12	879

Production started in 1969 with a total of 8,091, virtually all Jaguars and of course only in two forms, 2.8- and 4.2-litre. The peak year for production was 1971, with a grand total of 28,700 cars made, all six-cylinders.

In comparison with 98,000 XJs in five years it took Jaguar eight years to sell a total of 90,000 Mark IIs. Looking further, a total of 172,742 of all models (Mark II, 240/340, Daimler V8, "S" Type, 420, Sovereign, Mark

X/420G) were produced between 1960 and 1970 — an average of 17,000 cars a year. Bearing in mind that the XJ virtually replaced all other models, and that its average production was 19,600 per year, Jaguar certainly got their sums right.

What the Press said

The release of the 5.3-litre Series I XJ came as no surprise to the Press and the overall capabilities of the car impressed. One of the first magazines to cover the car was *Car and Driver* in October 1972, who stated, "It's not only the best Jaguar ever built . . . it may just be the best sedan available anywhere in the world".

The first British road test took place in March 1973 when *Autocar* put the XJ12 through its paces and found the new car had phenomenal performance but deplorable fuel consumption, comments that were subsequently echoed by other road testers as overall miles per gallon barely exceeded 11! With recorded acceleration figures of 0-60mph in 7 seconds and 0-100mph in 20.5 seconds, and a top speed of over 152mph, people who bought the XJ12 could forgive the car its excessive fuel consumption.

An *Autocar* 8,000-mile report on the car in 1974 revealed a series of faults. In the first few weeks minor, irritating complaints were noted like clonks from the transmission, a faulty power steering pipe causing loss of fluid, distortion in the laminated windscreen, ill-fitting driver's door, smell of petrol in the boot (a common complaint on XJs at the time), speedometer "rattle", incorrectly fitting and missing badges and some non-functioning instrument illumination.

Recurring coolant loss was finally traced to pressure loss through the overflow, necessitating the fitment of a catch tank. The petrol smells also continued until new type plastic petrol pipes were fitted in the boot, a service replacement subsequently fitted to all earlier cars.

At around 5,000 miles matters got more serious, with final drive oil leaks leading to the fitment of a new unit because of excessive noise. This was followed by more minor problems like replacing the boot seal and clock and rectifying a delay in the windscreen washer system. Within a further 2,000 miles an engine rattle was traced to a loose flange on the generator, a rear damper was replaced and adjustments to the Opus ignition system were needed to cure misfiring.

Although the car's many problems disappointed the driver, overall performance and handling were not in question. Nor apparently was the fuel consumption, better than expected at up to 14mpg.

Returning to the six-cylinder models, *Autocar* also carried out an 18,000-mile long-term report on the Series 1 4.2-litre saloon. Fuel consumption was considered reasonable at between 15 and 18mpg (not that much better really than the V12!) and the car behaved and looked like new at the end of the period. On delivery, however, various faults were identified. A strong smell of petrol was eventually rectified by modification at the factory. The fuel filter often became blocked, needing cleaning at 6,000-mile intervals. The body fared very well but the front doors dropped.

Series II and Coupé

"The Magic Formula XJ" proclaimed the first Series II brochure, enticing the reader to wander through the pages noting the

New driver controls
Revised interior
Safer braking
Laminated windscreen
Improved quietness
New heating and ventilation system
Fibre optic lighting
Restyled exterior . . .
. . and so on.

However, with the advent of the Series II saloons Jaguar's reputation as a quality car manufacturer deteriorated rapidly. Many reasons have previously been quoted for this condition, ranging from the British Leyland take-over to lack of morale in the workforce, poor quality control and poor quality parts from outside suppliers. It is not the writer's purpose to analyse the reasons but to comment on the outcome as far as the finished product was concerned — and there is no doubt that the Series II models had and to some extent still have a terrible reputation for unreliability and poor build quality, a situation that endured even through the introduction of the Series III models and into the initial period of Egan control.

Evidence of these problems can be seen in even the most well-kept and low-mileage examples today. Bodies on the whole were ill-prepared for painting; painting itself was of a very poor quality as was chrome plating, and the general fit of body panels was surprisingly bad even by the then BL standards, as seen on such cars as Marinas! Even small items such as door locks were of poor quality manufacture, and electrical problems (apparently endemic in XJs) were at their worst in Series II models.

Yet Series II cars are definitely Jaguars and drive, handle and perform just as XJs should. In researching this book I have seen and driven some beautiful examples which have stood the test of time despite the inherent problems of the model.

Good though the XJ Series I cars were and despite Jaguar's policy of updates and modifications they still had their flaws. Design changes were necessary to conform to new North American regulations and to overcome

some of the criticisms levelled at the early cars, so Jaguar decided that a new Series number was appropriate to a new and significantly improved model.

At the Frankfurt motor show on September 13th 1973 the Series II models were announced, along with a more sporting two-door version to be known as the XJC. Although the latter "C" (Coupé) models were officially released then, due to development problems the cars were not actually available until 18 months later, around April of 1975.

Dealing with the four-door models first, the 2.8-litre had already retired from the scene during Series I production, so this engine was never fitted in a Series II bodyshell, although still catalogued. The 4.2-litre six-cylinder and 5.3-litre twelve-cylinder units were still available for both Jaguars and Daimlers, although the V12 was not available in the short-wheelbase Series II saloon.

Six-cylinder cars received a new air cleaner assembly along with a thermostatically-controlled, exhaust-heated air intake system to reduce exhaust pollution. This outfit cut output to 170bhp at 4,500rpm. Allied to these changes, the exhaust flexible downpipes were eliminated in favour of a solid type merging into a double-skinned pipe splitting into separate silencers. A new Clayton Dewandre single-tube oil cooler was used, and the V12 type fan-cooled battery container was standardised on all models. Ventilated front disc brakes were now also standardised on all XJs, with modified pressure-differential wiring on the brake system to compensate for lack of pressure in one of the brake lines.

Styling mock-up for the Series II saloon at Browns Lane with full-width grille containing the inner headlights. Note also the vulnerable position of side lights/indicators.

For the V12 power unit there were few changes save for anti-pollution controls, which again adversely affected output, down to 250bhp.

One significant change for the Series II was in the heating and ventilating equipment, for despite steps forward by Jaguar in the Series I cars, the company had received too many complaints, particularly from export markets, about the ineffectiveness of the Jaguar system. Therefore an entirely new system, involving modifications of the bodyshell, was introduced on Series II and Coupé models.

The big advance was that instant variation of temperature was now afforded by the use of an air blending unit, as opposed to a conventional water system, effectively giving a two-temperature airflow facility. The temperature determined by the driver could be constantly maintained without regard to the speed of the car or the outside temperature. A very effective electric servo motor controlled various cams and gears to suit the climate required although engine vacuum still operated the air distribution flap and water valve to the heater unit. The integrated air conditioning system (still an extra cost option) was much more effective, with an output of 300cfm as opposed to 200 on Series I models. Twin electric fans either side of the bulkhead controlled the speed of airflow through the car.

A new single-skin bulkhead had to be designed to suit the new ventilation and heating system, with asbestos sealing to the engine side and Hardura pvc foam, felt and bitumen covering to the interior side: an ideal combination to reduce heat transference and noise from the engine bay. Allied to this, rigid pipes ran through the bulkhead, with flexible hoses connected either side for the heater, air con unit, etc., thus further reducing noise. These were easier to repair and replace than conventional fittings.

Jaguar also fitted effective flexible boots to the pedal box and steering column and even avoided the need for cables to pass through the bulkhead by using multi-pin sockets, eliminating holes in the bulkhead and making maintenance a lot easier. Specially moulded coverings were fitted to the bulkhead and floor to further insulate the interior from noise.

Both inside and out the Series II models were significantly different from the earlier cars. Externally, instant recognition from the front was easy, with the new bumper bar raised by some 4in to 16in, in line with North American Federal regulations — this also helped to make the frontal aspect smoother. The previous overriders were redesigned and became "underriders". (Due to Federal regulations US models featured rubber covered front and rear bumper bars.) With this change the below-bumper air intake became more prominent and the radiator grille shallower. The grille was standardised for all Jaguar models (although the V12 version did feature a simple black and gold plastic badge at the centre, and of course Daimler derivatives still had a ribbed top). Because the new grille had a more pronounced chromium-plated surround, Series II cars were more conventional and traditional looking in this respect, more pleasing to the eye, perhaps, than the rather "garish" Series I grille. Headlights remained unchanged but the side lights/indicators were now mounted below bumper level. These were of a new entirely plastic type, apparently giving them longer life (doubtful!), and were safer under impact. Finally at the front, and perhaps in recognition of changing laws on car safety, Jaguar fitted small rubber buffers above each underrider.

The side view was very little changed, though the keen eye would spot the higher front bumper level and the new "sculptured" wheels, either painted (or at extra cost) chromium-plated. V12 models also featured a neat coachline on the swage line of the car from front to rear, Daimler Vanden Plas versions still having a chromium-plated trim at this level. A couple of changes, not instantly noticeable, were made to provide extra safety for occupants: a laminated windscreen was now standard equipment on all cars, and all Series II doors featured two "W" section steel protection bars to guard against side impact.

Final styling of the Series II saloon was very neat and clean, with a frontal aspect that added to rather than detracted from the original XJ concept.

LEFT. The V12 Series II, the only telltale being the "V" badging in the centre of the grille. Note the Series II rubber buffers on the bumper bar, the pronounced underbumper grille and the discreet plastic side light/indicator housings.

TOP. North American Series IIs had rubber edged bumpers to meet Federal regulations. All US cars also featured front and rear sidemarkers (as on Series Is) and thin-band whitewall tyres.

ABOVE. Daimler and Jaguar 4.2-litre Series IIs: apart from the fluted grille and centre bonnet strip of the Daimler, both cars are identical from the front.

At the rear the only change amounted to the removal of the number plate light from bumper bar to a reasonably substantial chromium-plated plinth above the number plate (ribbed in the case of Daimler models). Again, rubber covered bumpers featured on US models. A heated rear screen was now standard equipment on all models.

The Series II bodyshell was actually 80lb heavier than the Series I, due in the main to the revised heater-ventilation system.

Inside, the Series II showed significant improvements, particularly in the ergonomics field. A new dashboard layout had been devised, with speedometer and rev counter still directly in front of the driver but now flanked by the four gauges for fuel, battery condition, oil pressure and water

Revised rear number plate
light treatment for the
Series II saloon.

temperature. A constant criticism of the new gauges concerned their bright yet cheap-looking surrounds. Between the two main 4in instruments a new multi-display panel was fitted, containing warning lights for main beam, hazard lights, ignition, parking brake, brakes (as on earlier Jaguars signifying loss of efficiency or low fluid level), oil pressure and seat belts. The row of centrally mounted identical rocker switches had been replaced by steering column mounted and ergonomically sited switchgear. Exterior lighting was now controlled by a large multi-function knob near the steering column, with a dipswitch/headlamp flash/direction indicator stalk mounted on the right of the steering column and a wiper/washer stalk on the opposite side (positions changing on left hand drive cars). The manual choke for the V12

Instruments, although very legible, had poor quality bright-finished bezels which looked cheap. The speedometer and rev counter were also of much smaller dimensions than on the Series I models. Note here that the bright trim has been continued to the fresh air outlets and elsewhere.

Totally revised dashboard treatment incorporating a large fresh air/air conditioning grille, and revised switching, instruments and steering wheel. On this particular car the leaping cat mascot on the centre grille and the under-dash mounted graphic equaliser are non-standard.

engine was still located under the dash panel as was the usual XJ ratchet pull-on handbrake near the centre console. The ignition/starter switch moved from the left of the steering column to the right.

In the centre of the dash panel a large plastic air-conditioning outlet grille was fitted, with smaller face-level ventilation outlets on the extreme right and left of the dash panel. A small flock-finished shelf was also featured in the centre of the dash panel, useful for parking meter change, tickets and the like. The passenger side glove box was much improved in size, eliminating the below-dashboard parcel shelf on each side of the car.

The centre console, although of similar design to the Series I item, now held the electric clock, flanked by oblong push-button switches for petrol tank changeover, map light, interior lighting and heated rear window, all on a satin finished panel. Below this were the radio and the heater/air conditioning controls, very much as on the previous models. The gear lever/automatic transmission quadrant and twin ashtrays were also unchanged, but the rocker switches further back on the centre armrest/cubby box were much larger and finished in black plastic, while an extra child safety cut-out switch prevented operation of the rear electric windows. Electric windows were available on all models. A point of interest on the dashboard was the use, for the first time in a car, of fibre optics to light the heating, air conditioning and lights switches. These high technology optics necessitated the use of 500 to 600 fibres in each millimetre of cable.

The front door trim panels were modified, having larger and more comfortable armrests with better grab handles, and the front quarterlights were now fixed to eliminate wind noise. The rear doors now contained separate ashtrays, and the earlier single ashtray on the rear of the centre console (susceptible to the "spray" of ash whenever the ventilator was open) was deleted. Inertia reel seat belts became standard equipment on all cars.

As a final touch Jaguar fitted a new twin-spoke steering wheel to all models, with a larger padded centre but of smaller overall dimensions

Centre console with
similar layout to earlier
models except for extra
switches for electric
windows in black
(previously finished in
chrome), cut-out switch
for rear windows and
central locking switch.
Note the rectangular
analogue clock and
switches, also new.

BELOW & BELOW RIGHT.
Series II saloon interior –
still very luxurious if not
so hard wearing in many
respects when compared
to the earlier cars.

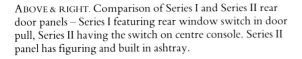

ABOVE & RIGHT. Comparison of Series I and Series II rear
door panels – Series I featuring rear window switch in door
pull, Series II having the switch on centre console. Series II
panel has figuring and built in ashtray.

(15½in). No horn ring was fitted, the horns being operated by pressure on any part of the padded area. Solenoid operated central locking was fitted for the first time, on all four doors (although not at this time on the boot), with a master switch on the centre console to lock all doors before getting out of the car, when the driver's door lock was automatically over-ridden.

Daimler models had all the same features as the Jaguars apart from the usual badging alterations, revised interior door trims, etc.

The XJC

As for the Coupé (or "C" models as they were properly known), these were a significant addition to the XJ line, being exceptionally stylish and a throwback to the pre-war days when William Lyons produced the SS Airline model, based on a saloon chassis but with a sleek pillarless two-door body. That particular car was not a great success and even Sir William did not number it among his favourites, but it is true to say that the XJC was his idea and much loved by him. Although not in production for very long it took significantly longer to develop than any other "improved" or "restyled" model. Coupés are already appreciating rapidly in value on the classic car scene today.

The bodyshell was based on the short-wheelbase XJ four-door saloon, but with only two doors of 4in longer length (and much heavier at nearly 200lb each!) than the standard cars, necessitating the use of strengthened door hinges. No front quarterlights or window frames were featured on Coupé models. Additional body strength was obtained by the use of a boxed pillar behind each door shut face, while the roof, also playing a part in the structural strength of the car, needed a slightly heavier rear panel between the rear screen and side windows. This was very effectively hidden by the black vinyl roof covering standard on all Coupés (except for a prototype once owned by the late Andrew Whyte). The vinyl covering also served the purpose of hiding imperfections in the steel roof pressings. The rear wings were obviously much longer on Coupé models, although retaining the general XJ shape. The Coupé bodyshell came out a good 50lb lighter than the original Series I four-door saloon.

Concept drawing for the Coupé, with Series I frontal treatment and wrap-around rear window.

An immaculate and
marvellously preserved
XJ6 4.2 Series II.

RIGHT. An XJ6 4.2 Series II, still in totally original condition, shows off its lines.

BELOW RIGHT. Series II frontal aspect showing raised bumper and under-bumper grille.

LEFT. XJ6 Series II interior.

LEFT. XJ6 4.2-litre Series II engine bay.

ABOVE. Series II Daimler
Vanden Plas with
chromium-plated wheels.

A concours winning
XJ6C, looking
purposeful.

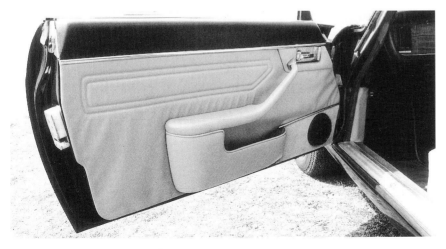

TOP. One of the early production Coupés on test prior to release.

ABOVE. Daimler XJ6C, one of the more common forms of Coupé, here seen with the optional Kent alloy wheels.

LEFT. Coupé door trim.

As the body was of pillarless construction it was desirable for all side windows to "disappear" from view when wound down. Electric window lifts were fitted to all windows and the rear windows had an ingenious mechanism: as the windows wound down they also tilted forward to avoid the rear wheelarch, thus disappearing into the body sides. Because of wind noise problems (always a worry on these Coupé models) Jaguar fitted a tensioned pulley system to keep the rear windows under pressure and effect a good seal against the door windows.

V12 Coupés always featured air conditioning as a standard feature.

All Coupé models were badged "C", e.g. XJ6C, XJ12C, and no other external changes were made.

Internally, the splendour of the Series II models was retained. The front seats tilted forward to provide (limited) access to the rear compartment, and the rear area was slightly diminished, but it was still very comfortable by two-door car standards. Even the inertia reel seat belts were well hidden, with their mechanisms fitted inside the rear side panels.

Coupé rear compartment.

Coupé interior.

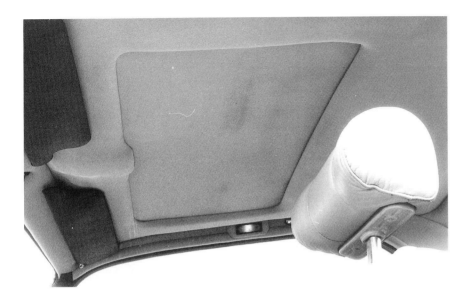

Factory-fitted sunroof on a Coupé. Note the sun visors, finished in black.

The Coupé was always a stylish and sought after model despite excessive wind noise and some degree of body flexing, which inevitably caused the doors to drop out of line. The model was never thought important by the Factory and perhaps never had a fair chance of success. BL never even gave it its own brochure. It is not hard to imagine that with individual colour schemes (like Vanden Plas) and better specifications it could have been a more lucrative and successful model.

Prices for the Series II saloons in 1973 were:

XJ6 Series II 4.2-litre manual/overdrive	£3,674
XJ6 Series II 4.2-litre automatic	£3,704
XJ6L Series II 4.2-litre manual/overdrive	£4,124
XJ6L Series II 4.2-litre automatic	£4,154
XJ12L Series II 5.3-litre automatic	£4,702

Although the Coupé versions were not actually available at this time due to labour problems and to production difficulties caused by ill-fitting doors and poor wind sealing, they were quoted on the Jaguar price list as follows:

XJ6C 4.2-litre automatic	£4,290
XJ6C 4.2-litre manual/overdrive	£4,260
XJ12C 5.3-litre automatic	£5,181

The Coupé models were clearly aimed at a specific area of the market up to that time dominated by the BMW 635 CSi and the Mercedes-Benz 450 SLC, both of which were significantly more expensive than the Jaguar. Other possible competitors at the time could have included the Lotus Elite, Aston-Martin V8 saloon, Bristol 412 and even the Rolls-Royce Corniche fixed head, all of which were also priced much higher than the Coventry-made cars.

As to colour schemes for the Series II models, one has to say that some of them were not at all what one might have expected from a quality manufacturer like Jaguar, not restrained, not sombre but probably fashionable and certainly individual! They were

Silver
Old English White
Regency Red (later changed to Damson although not for Coupés)
Sebring Red
Green Sand
Fern Grey
Sable (later changed to Carriage Brown)
Dark Blue
British Racing Green
Juniper Green
Lavender
Heather
Squadron Blue

The Series II models continued with various changes and modifications. In November 1973, due to a problem at the factory, XJ6 Series I wheel rims were being inadvertently fitted to the front hubs of Series II V12s — all were subsequently replaced. In December Jaguar decided to change over to a new Borg Warner automatic transmission, the Model 65, which became standard equipment on all six-cylinder models. The main reasons for the change amounted to a much smoother gear-change than on the previous Model 12 unit.

"A Jaguar is a Jaguar at any price" — the Series II 3.4

Much more significant was the introduction of a further version of the Series II in May 1975 — the 3.4-litre engined car.

Following the demise of the 2.8-litre Series I models, Jaguar still felt the need for a smaller-engined version. The increase in production would help keep down overall costs (a familiar ploy with Jaguar) and there were lucrative markets in Europe for a 3-litre sized engine, not to mention the possibility of fleet business in the UK. In search of this Jaguar even issued a brochure specifically geared to the fleet market headed "Jaguar XJ 3.4 — The Prestige Fleet Car". Quoting further from the same brochure, "What makes the XJ 3.4 a fleet car? For any company whose Directors' or Executives' cars have to reflect the success of the firm or status of the person, this Jaguar makes sound economic sense . . . competitively priced in comparison with other prestige saloons. Operating costs are contained by the Jaguar XJ 3.4's overall economy — particularly in overdrive form. " The white Series II 3.4 with green cloth upholstery featured in the brochure looked a stunning company car by any standards.

The 3.4-litre capacity was a throwback to earlier Jaguar days of the XK 120 and Mark VII and later the Mark II and 340. The bore and stroke remained the same as the old 3.4 engine's at 83 × 106mm, but the block was totally redesigned, with enlarged cooling passages and external ribbing to increase

ABOVE. The 3.4-litre saloon, virtually identical to its more expensive brothers save for 3.4 litre badging and the absence of some interior fittings.

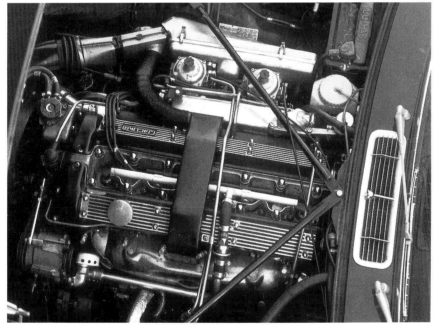

The 3.4-litre XJ6 (US spec) engine bay, showing warm air ducting from exhaust manifold to carburettors.

rigidity and strength. Grooved main bearings were used to increase oil flow. Twin SU HS8 carburetters were employed with an automatic choke and automatic temperature control for the air intake. In other respects the new 3.4-litre unit resembled the older engines in most ways but it was taller. The standard 4.2-litre straight port head was used, and output was virtually the same as the older 3.4-litre engine: 161bhp at 5,000rpm.

For the 3.4-litre models the gearbox was redesigned, with the bottom ratio lowered from 2.93 to 3.24:1 (also on the 4.2-litre cars). Reverse gear was lowered to 3.43:1 with an axle ratio of 3.54 to 1. Overdrive was standard equipment on manual cars, and automatic transmission was available utilising the Model 65 Borg Warner unit as then fitted to the 4.2-litre models.

The 3.4-litre car was deliberately priced low in the hope of increasing fleet sales, so electric windows were an extra-cost option and upholstery covering was in nylon anti-static stain resistant polyester, with narrow pleating, available in a limited choice of jade, sand, garnet, ruby or black. Although it was thought this new seat covering would be more durable than the traditional leather it was found to stain and mark easily and collected dust at an alarming rate! Kangol front seat belts were standard, of course, as on all models, but front seat head restraints were an extra-cost option.

The 3.4-litre engine was available in Jaguar and Daimler saloons but not in the Coupé (although at one time considered) or in the up-market Vanden Plas models. The only tell tales from the exterior that the car was a 3.4 was in the rear boot badging depicting "XJ 3.4", the lack of chromium-plated wheel Rimbellishers (an extra-cost option) and the absence of a coachline along the side of the body.

The 3.4-litre was never available in the USA and was initially launched in the UK at a price of £4,794 in automatic or manual/overdrive form. The price of the 4.2 was increased at this time to £5,136.

Listed extra-cost options for the 3.4 litre-Series II saloons were:

Tinted glass
Choice of radio and/or tape player
Rear compartment speakers for above
Metallic paint finish
Leather upholstery
Head rests
Rear seat belts
Electrically operated radio aerial
Chromium plated wheels
Chromium plated Rimbellishers
Whitewall tyres
Fog and spot lights

The Vanden Plas 4.2

Another new model based on the Series II XJ came in May of 1975: the 4.2-litre Vanden Plas, available in manual or automatic transmission form. All the refinements of the V12-engined Vanden Plas were to be found in the 4.2. A new and more sumptuous brochure was produced to "push" the Vanden Plas models, proclaiming "never have so many distinguished features combined so handsomely in a single car". The Vanden Plas models were conceived as being suitable for the wealthy owner/driver, or as a chauffeur-driven ceremonial carriage or a businessman's express. Vanden Plas cars had everything the Series II models had plus, as standard equipment:

Air conditioning system (new standard item for Series IIs)
Radio/cassette system (new standard item for Series IIs)
Distinctive metallic colour schemes
Hand finished paint

Chromium side mouldings with pin stripe
Black vinyl roof
Matching fog and spot lights
Individually shaped front and rear seats
Birstall Evlan carpets with heavier grade underfelt
Nylon over-rugs
Rear reading lamps
Red warning lights on doors
Special storage compartment in rear seat armrest
Wood veneer fillets with inlay on door trims
Tinted glass

The Vanden Plas was also modified to Series II specification, retaining its standard equipment extras plus, for the first time, chromium-plated ventilated wheels.

The other Daimler models at this time also received tinted glass and front seat head restraints as standard no-cost options.

Series II improvements

Another major development at the same time (May 1975) was the introduction of fuel injection for the V12 models, giving better economy, 14% more power, and reduced pollution, an important factor in the North American market. The fuel injection system was based on a Bendix design but made by Bosch and revised by Jaguar themselves with the help of Lucas. The fuel was injected directly into the inlet manifolds and the result was 285bhp at 5,750rpm.

The V12 power unit adapted to take fuel injection, here with the GM 400 automatic transmission.

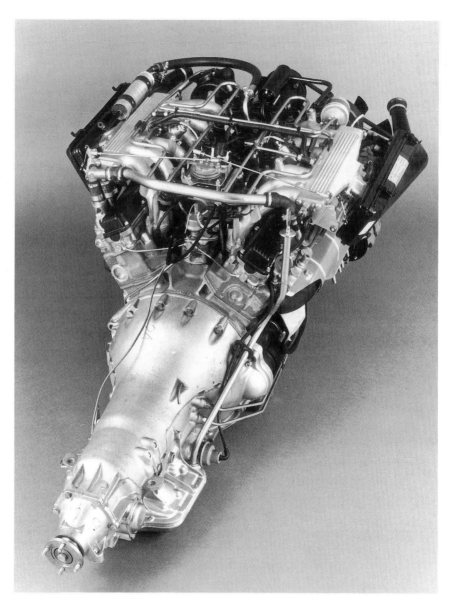

The electronic control unit was placed in the boot. Fuel supply was under pressure at 28psi to the injector nozzles, via a filter, and surplus pressure was released by a regulator valve and returned to the tanks. Fuel metering was regulated by four electronic control units, one a temperature sensor adjusting the fuel delivery from the injectors as required for the warm-up period, another controlling air temperature during normal running. At the manifold side of the throttle control a pressure sensor determined demand on the engine and lastly a throttle regulator measured the amount of throttle being used.

Initially fuel injection was only available on the Coupé models, the saloons soldiering on with carburettors until late 1975.

The V12's final drive ratio was changed from 3.3:1 to 3.07:1, giving 24.7mph at 1,000rpm compared to 22.9mph previously. This gave the V12 cars a genuine 100mph from only 4,050rpm. Six-cylinder models as well as

V12s also received at this time a revised steering rack with eight-tooth pinion, a revised anti-roll bar, a change in castor angle and amended upper wishbones to the front suspension, as well as a revised first gear ratio, lowered from 2.033 to 3.238:1. On the V12s alone a new rear main bearing side seal was fitted, with a harder crankshaft and greater bearing clearance. No other changes were made to the V12 power unit to accommodate fuel injection.

Visually the only clue to a V12 fuel-injected model was the adoption of a "fuel injection" logo on the boot, although GKN "Kent" alloy wheels were now available on 6in rims as an extra-cost item. Subsequently V12 saloons received a black vinyl roof in the same style as on Coupés along with a full length chromium-plated waist strip with accompanying pin stripe.

In May 1976 the existing HS type carburettors used on six-cylinder cars were replaced by a new HIF (Horizontal Integral Float chambers) type giving automatic adjustment of mixture strength according to the changes in temperature, effective from engine no. 8L.262204 on 4.2-litre engines.

In February 1977, due to complaints of premature carpet wear, particularly on the driver's side, Jaguar fitted better quality materials. Owing to reliability problems new type push switches for heated rear window, hazard lights, etc. were introduced (with new date code 47/76). Quality at this time was apparently a serious headache with far too much rectification work by main dealers needed on new vehicles both before and after delivery to customers.

In August many complaints were received about water leakage into the car. Many faults were found, some very common, including the roof drip rail being inadequately sealed to the roof panel (a problem later experienced on some Series IIIs as well), water lying in the "A" post lower box sections overflowing into the car via the footwells, and the battery tray collecting water from the bonnet gutter because of poor sealing. The heater/air conditioning unit also fared badly, with water entering via the blower motors and air conditioning condensation itself leaking into the footwells. On Coupés, water entered the rear seat panel area, with further problems around the rearmost sill drain hole allowing water to collect in the sill and the rear wings.

A significant change on all models was the fitting of another new automatic transmission in April 1977 in the form of the General Motors GM400 3-speed gearbox. This new unit, also used by many other luxury car manufacturers then and now (even Rolls-Royce), was of much sturdier construction to cope with the V12's torque, and offered much smoother gear changes.

Around the same time a four speaker Phillips radio/cassette AC460 system became available on Jaguars.

A sad period was to follow when in November 1977 the last two-door Coupés left the factory. Stopping Coupé production was a move necessary to increase production of four-door saloons, where demand constantly outstripped supply. The passing of the Coupé models was mourned by many, but Jaguar had never really got to grips with the problem of excessive wind noise. Incidentally, one example only of a Daimler Vanden Plas Coupé was produced, but apparently this model was never considered for serious production.

Total production of Coupés was:

XJ6C	6541
XJ12C	1862
Daimler Sovereign Coupé	1676
Daimler Double Six Coupé	408
Daimler Vanden Plas Coupé	1

In March 1978 six-cylinder engines received a new (non-interchangeable) oil filter assembly, new "O" rings in the air conditioning system to prevent leakage and avoid compressor failure, a Mullard amplifier for greater reliability, and new radiators for air conditioned cars. Twin electric radiator fans were introduced for the US, Australian and Japanese markets on air conditioned cars.

New, larger remote door mirrors were featured for all markets on the driver's side (except in Sweden and Japan), the side intrusion door members were deleted from all models (except in Japan and the USA) and the Alford and Adler power steering rack was changed on 3.4 and 4.2 models to the type then used in other vehicles of the Leyland fleet, the Princess and Triumph TR8.

Also on six-cylinder cars a revised 15psi pressure cap was used on the radiator, and improved Tuftrided exhaust valves were fitted from engine nos. 8L.51581 (4.2) and 8A.7841 (3.4).

In May 1978, due to the stricter pollution controls being forced not only on Jaguar but on every other luxury car manufacturer, the company decided to adapt the six-cylinder XK power units to fuel injection. The Lucas/Bosch L-Jetronic system was used with a 3-way catalytic converter. Larger inlet valves were employed, of 1.875in instead of 1.75in, and the compression ratio was increased from 7.8:1 to 8:1; with this bhp increased to 176 from 161 with better fuel consumption. One big advantage of the new fuel injection six-cylinder engines was that the same unit was used for all markets, thus facilitating production.

In July 1978 cosmetic changes took place. The side light housings were converted to single operation as indicator tell-tales, with full width amber lenses accordingly. The side lights were moved to become pilot lamps within the main outer headlamp units. Because of changes in EEC regulations new Vin numbers (vehicle identification number) were introduced, situated on a new style plate on the front right hand side of the engine compartment; these Vin numbers replaced the previous chassis numbers. Internally, the centre console finishers, usually of bright aluminium, were changed to black (a one-piece finisher only). Similarly, due to comments about the cheap and nasty bright plastic surrounds to the instruments, air vents, etc, these were changed.

By August 1978 Jaguar had finally identified the reason why the horn could sound without the horn push being pressed. It was found that in heavy rain water passed between the scuttle and wiper box sealing rings, filling a depression in the bulkhead. When cornering the water ran down into the horn earth connection in the steering column, causing a short circuit which made the horns sound. A sealer was applied between the sealing rings and the scuttle to stop water getting in.

In September, 3.4- and 4.2-litre engines received a disposable oil filter canister — the previous type had a tendency to split. The later type is white in colour without the usual finger flaps, and was fitted from engine nos. 8L.70840 (4.2) and 8A.101372 (3.4). The V12 dipstick tube was found to be faulty, coming away from its mounting easily, and an improved fixing was employed. At the same time window lift electric motors were replaced by a heavy duty type to improve reliability.

By October more complaints had prompted Jaguar to take action on poor window sealing, water leaks, etc. An agreed strategy was sent out to all dealers requesting full and proper evaluation of the problem by the following method:

Testing of car must be done with an observer in the passenger seat at speeds of between 50 and 70mph. A strip of paper about 1in wide to be used to verify that proper seals are being made between door frames and body. The paper to be pinched between the frame and body while the doors are closed. A firm contact should be made in all areas where seals are made. Most causes of such wind noise come from:

"A"Post Joggle — Sealing of the "A" post where two panels overlap leaving a "step". In drastic cases the "step" needing smoothing out, filling and repainting.

"A" Post Profile — The gaps between door and doorframe needing adjustment.

Tooling Holes — Holes in panels needing adequate filling and sealing against wind noise.

Glass Innerdraft Seals — In some cases incorrectly fitted or short in length.

Quarterlights — Incorrect sealing of quarterlight areas.

Window Frame Misshape — Adjustment of window frame to bow in or out to effect proper seal against body upper half.

In February 1979, due to new UK/European regulations, it was necessary to fit speedometers for all markets with joint mph/kmh calibration. This procedure was carried out at the factory although many cars were "still in the field" with dealers because of slow sales. It was therefore necessary to change speedometers on all the unsold cars. The new speedometers also differed in containing the rear screen heater warning light, which had been in the rev counter, and in incorporating a bulb failure warning light which for the Series II cars remained unused.

In March 1979 the XJ six-cylinder models were rebadged, becoming "XJ 3.4", "XJ 4.2", etc., except for the US market where "XJ 6" continued (the 3.4-litre car was never available in the USA anyway).

Even as late as April 1981 Jaguar were still listing complaints of water ingress and wind noise, and in that month they released sets of revised door seals for Series I and Series II long-wheelbase models under part nos.:

right hand front	RTC 2610
left hand front	RTC 2609
right hand rear	RTC 2612
left hand rear	RTC 2611

It was unfortunate for Jaguar and Daimler that during the time of the Series II cars and British Leyland ownership the two marques started to lose not only control over their destiny but also their prestige. BL badges started to appear on some cars, and group brochures were put out featuring all models from the Daimler Vanden Plas down to the humble Triumph Dolomite 1300.

Series II production

Despite all these problems Jaguar continued to turn out record numbers of cars (although not always of the highest quality) with totals for the Series II of:

	four-door	two-door
Jaguar 3.4/4.2	77,500	6,541
Daimler 3.4/4.2	20,075	1,676
Jaguar V12	16,060	1,862
Daimler V12	4,292	408

The peak year of Series II production was 1974, with a grand total of 28,871 cars. Series II production as a whole represented a 20,000-unit increase over the Series I (disregarding the Coupé versions). Production finally ceased in March 1979, by which time the basic price of a 4.2-litre had risen to nearly £10,000. It was time for the Series II saloons to make way for the next generation of XJs, the Series III.

What the Press said

Although Jaguar had not allowed the 2.8-litre Series I out for road testing, the 3.4-litre Series II received a British road test in the pages of *Motor* in September 1975. The writer found that despite a lack of torque and acceleration the car was as smooth as ever and quite willing to cruise effortlessly at the legal speed limit. Performance was definitely up on the earlier 2.8-litre car, with good fuel consumption recorded, up to 23 miles per gallon at a steady speed. Despite the changes in the heating and ventilation system this still did not find favour with *Motor*, nor did some of the more archaic left-overs from the earlier days like the "dancing" wiper mechanism.

When comparing the 3.4-litre with the competition, *Motor* chose the BMW 528, Mercedes-Benz 280E, Opel Commodore, Rover 3500S and Volvo 264. Only the Rover was really cheaper, the BMW was virtually the same price, and the others were substantially more than the Jaguar 3.4-litre price of £4,998. On the 0-60mph sprint the Jaguar was virtually the slowest — even half a second behind the Volvo, not known for its performance — but on top speed the Jaguar beat the Volvo at 113mph compared with 104. On fuel consumption, however, the Jaguar was at 20mpg, the Rover second and the Volvo bottom.

In their road test of the Series II 4.2-litre XJ in 1978 *Motor* compared the car with the BMW 728, Ford Granada 2.8i Ghia, Mercedes-Benz 280SE, Rover 3500 and Volvo 264 (perhaps in the latter two cases a fairer comparison than with the 3.4-litre Jaguar earlier). By this time the XJ6 had increased in price to £9,753, nearly £2,000 dearer than the very well equipped though not so prestigious Ford Granada, and overall the dearest car in the comparison. There was little between the cars in top speed (though the Volvo was much slower). On acceleration (again leaving out the Volvo) the Jaguar only rated fifth with 0-60mph in 10.6 seconds. However, on general handling, ride and smoothness the XJ6 outperformed the competition, despite its near ten-year-old design, although *Motor* keenly picked up many "period" points that gave away the Jaguar's age when compared with most of the competition.

In a comparative test alongside a Mercedes-Benz 450SEL, Ford LTD (American) and Holden Caprice (Australian) the V12 Jaguar was the fastest on acceleration and top speed although not at all competitive on fuel consumption, even when compared with the big American Ford. In another comparison, with the Rolls-Royce Silver Shadow II, Ferrari just pipped the Jaguar to fastest outright speed, and the XJ was third on acceleration from 0-60mph, at 7.8 seconds, compared with the Aston Martin at 6.2 seconds and Ferrari at 7.1 (although both the latter did have manual transmission). Surprisingly, it wasn't the worst on fuel consumption, beating the Aston and the Ferrari! Putting the test in true context the Jaguar did only cost £12,436 compared with the nearest-priced (and not so well equipped) BMW at £12,699, the others being well out of the Jaguar price bracket.

The Coupé, particularly in V12 form, was well liked by the Press. Despite the shorter wheelbase and slightly restricted access and rear seating, all found the Coupé a very practical car. Rivals at the time were few, save for perhaps the Lotus Elite at around the same price as a V12 Coupé, the BMW 635CSI at £4,000 more, the Mercedes-Benz 450SLC at £5,000 more, the Aston Martin V8 at nearly £16,600 or the Bristol 412 at over £20,000. The Lotus, although an excellent sports car, did not have anything like the refinement or finish of the Jaguar, and the Aston and Bristol at substantially higher prices were arguably in a different and more select class, but the BMW and Mercedes were of similar dimensions and performance and slotted well into the Jaguar market. However, at nearly 50% high prices they did not offer the excellent value for money for which the Coventry-built product has always been known.

It is interesting to note that in 1980 *Old Motor* magazine carried out a resumé of the cars of the seventies; the V12 Jaguar was undoubtedly to them the Car of the Decade, though at that time of the OPEC crisis they did feel that all V12s and in particular the Jaguar with its poor fuel consumption were "an endangered species". Little did they realise that over eleven years later the V12 would still be going strong!

In *Old Motor* of February 1982 the V12 Coupé was earmarked as "The Car to Keep" — advice that may have been a little premature then, but since that time the Coupé Jaguar has increased nicely in value.

The Final Phase — Series III and the XJ Revival

"Success breeds success — The World's Finest Saloon".

Whilst the Series II XJ must be considered an advance in engineering over the original Series I car, there was no doubt that by 1977 the model range needed revitalisation in a big way. Contemporary road tests of the XJ saloons were always favourable but there were many (if often minor) criticisms.

Jaguar needed to boost sales and their image in the luxury saloon market and therefore set about a £7-million investment plan to redesign the existing XJ saloons, with the aid of Pininfarina from Turin in Italy — the first time that Jaguar had felt it necessary to enlist the help of a "foreign" styling studio with design. A brand new £15½-million body and paint plant had

XJ Series III production line around 1978-79.

70

been commissioned by Pressed Steel Fisher in Castle Bromwich (later to become Jaguar's own body plant) and they made use of these excellent new facilities for the Series III saloons. With such intricate processes as phosphate pre-treatment, electro priming, the use of an adhesion promoter and no less than four coats of thermo-plastic acrylic colour, a much improved finish was guaranteed. Although widely publicised upon the launch of the Series III, these processes did not enter the production process until around October 1981, which meant that many of the earlier cars of this Series were used to experiment with different types of paint processes, and many problems were experienced. Undersealing was provided, with wax injection into box sections, although here again a full injecting process was not introduced until around October 1982.

The Series III models were released on 29th March 1979, some ten years on from the original XJ concept, and the new cars put Jaguar back in the forefront of design of luxury motor vehicles.

Two coats of lacquer complete the clear-over-base paint process announced on the release of Series III, though this process was not employed until later in the model's life.

One of the first press pictures taken of the Series III XJ6. Note the revised frontal treatment with thick rubber bumper incorporating the indicator lights, much larger window area, flatter roof and sculptured stainless steel wheel trims.

Although mechanically very much a Series II model, the Series III incorporated mostly new body panels and better trim and equipment. Most noticeable was the increased glass area (the knowledgeable may well recall a similar transition from the Mark I saloon to the Mark II model). The windscreen had 3in extra rake, the rear screen was flatter and the side windows were deeper. All glass was now tinted as standard equipment (except on 3.4-litre models where it was an extra-cost option) and the front screen as well as being laminated was bonded to the bodyshell by a thermal process, providing extra rigidity to the shell.

The new Series III XJ12 sporting Kent alloy wheels, headlamp wash/wipe and twin coachlines.

The roofline of the Series III cars was raised approximately 3in at the rear both to accommodate the extra glass area and to provide more rear passenger headroom. Overall height remained the same as on earlier cars but miraculously the Series III looked lower and flatter.

ABOVE. Daimler Double Six Series III. Note the old-style Kent alloy wheels

XJ6 4.2 Series III looked, but was not, smaller than its predecessor.

ABOVE AND RIGHT. XJ6 3.4 Series III, one of the last made, in pristine condition and with the optional pepperpot alloy wheels.

Series III XJ6 3.4 interior.

BELOW. The 3.4 Series III
engine, still using twin
SUs.

ABOVE. Series III
production line at Browns
Lane, Coventry in 1978.

BELOW. In goes the
engine, complete with
gearbox and exhaust
downpipe.

The basic styling remained unmistakeably XJ although the 'Coke bottle' hump over the rear wing was now less pronounced. From the front and rear the overall appearance was significantly altered by the use of rubber-faced injection moulded bumpers on all models (export and home market), although for the US market 5mph absorption units of Menesco telescopic sections on an aluminium frame were fitted which however looked exactly the same as the UK versions. To add extra finish to the rubber bumpers (which now incorporated flasher units at the front and high intensity fog lights at the rear except on US market cars) chromium-plated top covers were provided. The front bumper also accommodated space for the number plate. A new style of chromium-plated radiator grille was employed, common to all Jaguar models but with a gold-on-black Jaguar head for six-cylinder models and gold-on-beige for V12s (but without any specific V12 markings). For Daimler models a fluted grille virtually identical to the Series II type was used. Headlight treatment remained the same except that the side lights were incorporated in the outer units as on the last Series IIs. At

Comparison of Series I V12 and Series III V12 clearly shows the later car's lower look. Note the much increased window area of the later model, the lack of front quarterlights and the flush mounted door handles.

Rear view of the Series III clearly shows the new lighting treatment.

the rear there was a revised number plate housing (different for the Daimler models in that they were fluted). Larger rear light units were used, now incorporating the reversing lights.

Badging at the rear and side was also revised. At the rear the script "Jaguar" (or "Daimler") was always to the left of the number plate with, to the right of the number plate, the model designation: XJ6 3.4, XJ6 4.2 or XJ12 5.3. On Daimler derivatives the word Sovereign appeared to the right, with the designation 4.2 or Double Six 5.3. The only excursion from this method was on the Vanden Plas models, where the Vanden Plas badging was on the right with the 4.2 or 5.3 emblem on the left. Badging was featured on the sides of the front wings as before except that 3.4-litre models wore badges finished in silver on black, 4.2s and 5.3s gold on black.

From the side view, the new Series III V12 had a double coachline, the 4.2 a single coachline and the 3.4 no coachline at all, although this was always available as an extra-cost option at the time of ordering. Conventional 6K road wheels were employed, with stainless steel hub caps incorporating exposed wheel nuts. Alternatively alloy wheels could be ordered at extra cost for all models except the Vanden Plas, on which they were standard equipment.

At the front, quartz halogen headlights were standard equipment on all models (except the 3.4-litre) and a revised front valance was fitted plus, of course, the new rubber bumper treatment. Headlamp wash-wipe systems using miniature wiper blades and working on the outer lamp units only were an extra-cost option for 4.2- and 5.3-litre cars (standard on Vanden Plas and USA models) but not available at all on 3.4s. They were controlled by the washer/wiper stalk on the steering column and were provided with washer jets; the washer system needed and got a larger 12½ pint water reservoir in the nearside wing.

Internally the Series III cars were much improved in all manner of respects. The seats were redesigned with backs raised by 1½in for better overall support. Lumbar support adjustment was provided for the front seats, allowing up to 1½in of movement to harden or soften the backrest according to individual requirements. This was standard on all models, as was a new style of headrest with better shaping and closer to the body. Electric front seat adjustment for both front seats was provided as standard equipment on Vanden Plas models, carried over from the Series II model (where it was an option). It was controlled by a chromium-plated switch on the door side of each seat. On other models electric adjustment of the driver's seat only could be had as an extra-cost option. The system did not incorporate height adjustment as on cars like Rolls-Royce but merely gave fore-and-aft and tilt adjustment. All Series III models featured map pockets in the backs of the front seats.

Inertia reel seat belts were a standard fitment on all models, discreetly hidden behind the B/C post trim panels. Rear passenger seat belts were an option on all models although standard on cars destined for France, Canada and the USA.

A new padded cloth, glass-fibre backed headlining was fitted, with recessed sun-visors moulded to shape and finished in a contrasting colour (usually black). A larger rear view mirror was also fitted. Interior courtesy lights now stayed on for up to 15 seconds after the doors were closed, allowing the driver time to find the ignition lock in the dark.

New deep-pile carpeting of a higher quality than before also provided better sound deadening and gave a more "expensive" feel to the whole interior of the car. Coupled with this was a sandwich of sound deadening materials laid inside the body and boot. A half-inch layer of foam with a ³/₁₆in lining lay beneath the carpet. Colour options for carpets were limited to

The luxurious interior of the Series III saloon with much improved seats, revised steering wheel and modified dashboard treatment.

75

dark blue, russet red, light brown and black.

Although the dashboard was of the same layout as on the Series II cars, minor amendments had been made to improve the design and engineering. The revised steering wheel, cloth covered, had a central, horizontal spoke allowing the main instruments to be viewed easily when travelling in a straight line. The dash switch labelling was replaced by the new international symbols (eliminating the need for Jaguar to change legends for different markets). Along with this, improved graphics were used on the speedometer and rev counter and new warning lights were included in the speedometer and rev counter for such items as bulb failure warning, etc. The steering column stalks were changed over, with the indicators on the left and washer/wiper on the right, apparently to fall in line with continental practice. Twin electric chromium-plated "joysticks" could be fitted to control the door mirrors, this feature being standard on Vanden Plas and US models, optional on others. If these were not specified, conventional cable operated mirrors were fitted as on the Series IIs. A better quality radio or radio/cassette system was fitted manufactured by Phillips (the AC 460am mono system on 3.4s and 4.2s, AC 860fm stereo system for V12s, Daimlers and Vanden Plas models) with four speakers (one in each door). A standard equipment electric aerial was mounted on the rear wing, with delayed retraction after switching off the radio or engine. On cars destined for the US market a separate aerial switch was incorporated allowing the driver to select exact aerial height to suit the masses of individual FM stations available. The rear screen heater was fitted with a timer that cut off automatically after 15 minutes.

An entirely new central locking system was fitted to Series IIIs which for the first time included electro-locking of the boot with one operation. Three keys were provided, one operating the ignition only, one a service key that fitted the ignition and doors, and a third master key that fitted the boot and glove compartment also. This procedure was in line with practice on many other luxury cars of the period.

The windscreen wiper mechanism was also amended and brought up to date after may minor complaints, mainly from magazine road testers. The wipers now parked automatically without the famous "dancing around" performance reminiscent of many 50s and 60s British cars! An intermittent wash/wipe facility was also added, with a six-second delay built in. The wipers now parked on the opposite side, eliminating the unwiped areas in the driver's field of vision, a fault on all previous XJs.

It is worth at this point giving some technical detail of the Econocruise Speed Control System adapted from the Series II models and now available as an extra-cost option on all Series III automatic transmission cars. Originally developed in the USA it was to become a "required option" on most luxury vehicles, and Jaguar could not ignore the potential to increase sales by making this option available on XJ saloons. By the use of a sophisticated yet very reliable electronic control unit the system can record a predetermined speed and adjust the throttle opening to maintain that speed. Memory circuits will re-establish the speed if the driver disengages the system either manually (through an on/off switch on the centre console near the transmission quadrant) or automatically upon request (by the use of a "Resume" control) if the system disengages through either switching off the engine, applying the brakes or operating the accelerator. The desired speed can be set by a push-button control on the left steering column stalk. Although very sophisticated the system rarely gives trouble. It involves four switches (the "set" switch on the column stalk, a "brake" switch to automatically disengage the system, the "master" switch for on/off/resume control and the "gear inhibit" switch eliminating the use of the cruise control in any gear other than drive. Also incorporated are the control unit, the speed transducer controlling the speed, and the actuator controlling the pulses from the control unit and allowing the manifold vacuum to pull open the throttle.

The boot now contained a much more traditional and ostentatious briefcase to hold the tool kit. This contained:

Six spanners
Multi-screwdriver
Pliers
Spare bulbs
Tyre gauge
Spare plug
Fuses
Sockets

As a final touch, better quality sound deadening padding was used all round the car, including pre-formed rubber/foam panels to the doors, bulkhead and propshaft tunnel.

Mechanically the new cars were little changed except that the Rover SD1 five-speed gearbox was introduced, with a new casing, stronger 77mm layshaft, bigger bearings and altered ratios to cope with the additional power of the Jaguar six-cylinder models. These modifications

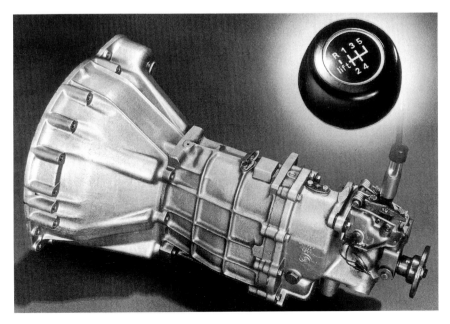

The Rover-based five-speed gearbox offered in the Series III six-cylinder saloons, complete with BL logo on the casing!

The 4.2-litre XK engine in the Series III shell.

had apparently already been completed for Police Rovers prior to fitting in Jaguar cars. The new fifth gear (replacing overdrive) gave 25.8mph at 1,000rpm in top gear. Unfortunately no manual transmission V12s were to be available.

The six-cylinder 4.2-litre engine now developed 19% more power: 205bhp at 5,000rpm, with torque up from 222 to 236lb/ft. 4.2s were now equipped with a Lucas/Bosch L-Jetronic sealed fuel injection system and a new air cleaner system to cut down intake noise levels. They also featured a fuel cut-off on the overrun; as the accelerator was released the fuel supply would be cut off until 1,200rpm had been reached. Compression ratio was raised to 8.7:1 through the use of E Type 9:1 cr pistons and the extra space taken by the bigger inlet valves ($1\frac{7}{8}$in instead of $1\frac{3}{4}$in). The inlet valves opened earlier at 22° before top dead centre instead of 17°. On the V12s a higher pressure fuel system was fitted giving 36psi.

The 3.4-litre model remained mechanically the same as before, with twin SU carburettors. V12s continued with the Lucas/Bosch D-Jetronic fuel injection system.

Despite the Leyland presence at Jaguar and complaints about poor build quality and unreliability, the company was selling the Series III cars very successfully, although the choice of colour schemes on these early cars was severely limited, for such a high quality luxury saloon, to Tudor White, Cotswold Yellow and Damson Red, with Beige and Brown added a few months later. Jaguar continued to work on a programme of improvement for the model range that started in May 1980 with the elimination of the 3,000-mile service interval, replacing this with a much more realistic interval of 7,500 miles. The 12,000-mile service interval was extended to 15,000. This made a lot more sense against the competition of the day.

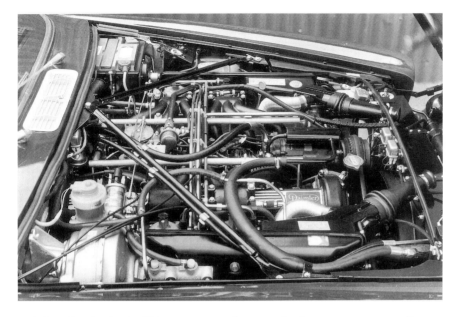

V12 engine in Series III shell, with complex fuel injection system and piping for air conditioning.

Prices for the Series III cars were unfortunately, but not unexpectedly, up on the Series II prices:

XJ6 3.4-litre	£11,189
XJ6 4.2-litre	£12,326
XJ12 5.3-litre	£15,015
Daimler Sovereign 4.2-litre	£12,983
Daimler Double Six	£15,689
Daimler Vanden Plas 4.2-litre	£17,208
Daimler Vanden Plas 5.3-litre	£20,277

Extra-cost options for the majority of models, although some were standard on Vanden Plas and export cars, included (with some indications of prices):

Automatic transmission
Air conditioning (£988)
Tinted glass
Electric sunroof (£461)
Phillips stereo cassette/radio system (£210)
Cloth trim (4.2 and 5.3 only)
Leather trim (3.4 only)
Rear head restraints
Rear seat belts (£59)
Alloy wheels (£410)
Matching rectangular fog and spot lamps
Quartz halogen headlamps (3.4 only)
Twin electric door mirrors (£92 each)
Adjustable reading lamps in rear compartment
Headlamp wash/wipe system (£164)
Cruise control, auto transmission cars only (£256)
Driver's seat height adjustment, electric (£150)

Colour schemes later developed to include:

Exterior	Interior	Carpet	Coachline
Tudor White	Russet leather	Red	Gold
	Biscuit leather	Light brown	Gold
	Garnet cloth	Red	Gold
	Sand cloth	Light brown	Gold
Cotswold Yellow	Cinnamon leather	Light brown	Copper
	Dark blue leather	Grey	Copper
	Sand cloth	Light brown	Copper
	Navy cloth	Grey	Copper
Damson Red	Russet leather	Red	Gold
	Cinnamon leather	Light brown	Gold
	Garnet cloth	Red	Gold
	Sand cloth	Light brown	Gold
Silver Frost	Russet leather	Red	Copper
	Dark blue leather	Grey	Copper
	Garnet cloth	Red	Copper
	Navy cloth	Grey	Copper
Cobalt Blue	Cinnamon leather	Light brown	Gold
	Dark blue leather	Grey	Gold
	Sand cloth	Light brown	Gold
	Navy cloth	Grey	Gold
Racing Green	Biscuit leather	Light brown	Gold
	Cinnamon leather	Light brown	Gold
	Sand cloth	Light brown	Gold
Quartz Blue	Biscuit leather	Light brown	Gold
	Dark blue leather	Grey	Gold
	Sand cloth	Light brown	Gold
	Navy cloth	Grey	Gold
Chestnut Brown	Biscuit leather	Light brown	Gold
	Cinnamon leather	Light brown	Gold
	Sand cloth	Light brown	Gold
Sebring Red	Biscuit leather	Light brown	Copper
	Dark blue leather	Grey	Copper
	Sand cloth	Light brown	Copper
	Navy cloth	Grey	Copper
Black	Russet leather	Red	Gold
	Biscuit leather	Light brown	Gold
	Garnet cloth	Red	Gold
	Sand cloth	Light brown	Gold

Sebring Red and Black were non-standard colours available at extra cost. Apart from these no other colours were available at all, even to special order, although black as a leather interior trim (or ebony in the case of cloth) was available with grey carpets to special order at extra cost. Special colours were offered for Vanden Plas models as before.

Upon the release of the Series III XJ saloons Jaguar were keen to promote their heritage and pedigree, and devoted a large part of the original brochures to a brief history of the marque (including the Le Mans racing successes). As a result of BL's problems Jaguar's fortunes were declining, and it was important to project the quality both of the cars and of the production methods. Here again the brochure, produced in lavish colour to a larger than normal format, gave a vast amount of space to pictures of the cars during production, details of the painstaking methods adopted by the Company (specially imported leather hides from Scandinavia, intricate matching of veneers, etc.), and listing many of the tests and checks that all cars went through before being released from the line, for example:

- Bores in the cylinder blocks checked to the finest limits.
- Craftsmen balance the pistons and conrods into precisely matching sets.
- Every engine bench tested for at least 1 hour.
- Piping in the engine compartment and brake systems checked, as are all vital bolts and nuts.
- Paintwork checked for any blemishes or irregularities both before and after assembly, up to eight times in all.
- Hides and later seating seams checked for small flaws.
- Dashboard checked minutely for the match of the twin veneers, and the positioning of the instrumentation.
- Wheels and tyres all checked including the spare.
- Electrical systems checked, including interior and exterior lighting.
- First road test, operating of car and controls verified, such items as rear axle and underside checked.
- Second road test, tester given free hand to find any fault, however small.
- Final check on trim inside and ensure car is immaculate before it leaves the factory.

Enough tests and controls, one would think, to ensure the utmost quality in any Jaguar produced. Unfortunately, as we now all know, these tests were not enough, and although in concept the Series III cars were truly remarkable, in quality control and finish a lot was left to be desired.

For the Daimler brochures Jaguar revived a more individual approach used for the Series I Sovereigns. Colour photographs were commissioned from famous photographers like Lichfield and Bailey, each shot individually captioned, "Photograph by . . . , Masterpiece by Daimler".

Improving the breed

By June 1979 changes were already afoot to improve the Series III cars, starting with complaints of premature interior light lens discoloration and melting caused by the use of 10 watt bulbs, these being amended on all future models to 6 watt. In July the swept area of the windscreen was improved by the fitting of a lengthened driver's wiper arm of 368mm, the passenger side remaining at 356mm. In the same month, for 5.3-litre cars, an improved radiator was fitted with major internal core modifications, increasing the depth of weld to avoid any possibility of blockage through a build-up of debris (effective from Vin No. 100770). Revised handbooks were printed for V12s as the previous Series III books had contained incorrect information on tyre size: ER70 VR 15 should have read 205 70 VR 15. Also in July instructions went out to all dealers to modify the driver's side floor carpet, cutting a slit adjacent to the accelerator mounting; it had been found that removal of this portion of the carpet involved time-consuming dismantling of the accelerator spring clip, in many cases incorrectly refitted afterwards.

By August 1979 those models equipped with headlamp wash/wipe systems benefitted from a new style flat-faced Lucas H4 177.8mm Halogen headlamp unit, subsequently fitted to earlier cars as the previous domed glass type was proving unsuitable for wash/wipe operation. Because of complaints from owners who had forgotten to switch off their side lights, new rheostat switches were incorporated for the instrument lighting with a minimum brightness stop (so that the illumination could not be switched off entirely), effective from Vin no. 302107.

In September 5.3-litre cars received a new AB3 electronic ignition amplifier of smaller dimensions to improve accessibility to engine components. It was now sited on the radiator crossmember, from Vin no. 111703. Earlier cars could not be retrospectively modified in this way. V12s also received a revised downpipe catalyst assembly with two-bolt manifold-to-downpipe fitting instead of four-bolt. Because of front and rear screen seal failure a new direct glazing method was employed on all models, as used on the Rover SD1 and Triumph TR8 models.

In October a revised 3.4-litre engined XJ6 was made available at £500 below the then price, deliberately aimed at increasing sales in the very price-conscious fleet market. No changes were made to the 3.4-litre specification and it was still possible to build up the price of a 3.4-litre car with the option of the regular XJ6/12 features such as electric windows, leather upholstery, etc. Unfortunately this did very little to actually boost sales of the 3.4. At this time new Pirelli P5 205 70 VR15 tyres (blackwall only) became available alongside the Dunlops, and were made standard equipment for the North American market. Complaints of fuel pump noise from the boot were found to be due to the pump being in direct contact with the boot floor, rectified by the fitment of padding. On 3.4 and 4.2 cars cam follower guides were coming loose, particularly on the exhaust bank, so the interference fit between the head and tappet guide was increased by .0125mm from engine no. 8L.86791 (4.2) and 8A.86791 (3.4).

Still in 1979, in November owners were complaining of boot interior lights remaining on even when the boot was closed. This was remedied on all subsequent models (from Vin no. 306136) by adjustment ensuring the light was extinguished 2in before the boot closed. To provide increased coolant transfer between the cylinder block and head on six-cylinder cars, slotted waterways were introduced between the cylinder bores corresponding with additional waterways in the cylinder head. If fitting this later block with an earlier head, drilling must be carried out to match the waterways.

Finally, in December 1979 for the 1980 model year, colour options were extended with the addition of extra-cost special colours to the range:

Brazilia
Atlantis
Dark Green

Vanden Plas colour schemes were also amended to:

Silver Sand Metallic
Caramel Metallic
Coral Metallic
Biascan Blue Metallic
Mistletoe Metallic
Mink Metallic
Amethyst Metallic

Interior trim colours were very varied at this time with a choice of:

Cloth	Sand
	Garnet
	Navy
	Ebony
Leather	Cinnamon
	Biscuit
	Russet
	Dark blue
	Black
	Grey

Vanden Plas special trim colours were tan, chamois and deep olive.

In January 1980 Jaguar decided to delete one of the engine mounting spacers (part no. C.30721) to give better underbonnet clearance for the engine. Headlamp rims were changed to allow headlamp adjustment without removing the rim on export cars. After complaints from dealers about paint flaking on the door handles, on all models from Vin no. 306850 improved matt black polyester powdered paint was used. In the interior, improved trim stitching appearance was gained through the use of trim-coloured thread. On the tyre front, Dunlop modified the bead seat angle to improve "out of round" characteristics, giving better vibration control particularly when the tyres were part worn. These new tyres were easily identifiable by the letter "N" moulded into the sidewall after the word "radial". On 5.3s the Dunlop SP sport tyres were replaced by new Supersport D7s.

In March, after problems experienced with the Silver Frost metallic paint finish, a new type acrylic with two coats of clear overlay lacquer was introduced.

In September, due to complaints of water entering the door speakers via the window channels, special speaker shields were added to the interiors of all doors from Vin no. 310610.

From October the driver's footwell carpet was supplied in two distinct pieces to simplify production, from Vin no. 317139. At the same time due to major problems with Damson paint finishes caused by reaction with thinners during spraying, a new formulation for the colour was devised. From Vin no. 319125 an anti-chip paint finish was used on outer sills and front and rear valances to combat problems with premature corrosion.

In November a new Merlin flush-fitting aerial arrived, replacing the Radiomobile type from Vin no. 316035, this action being taken due to problems with reliability in the old unit.

For 1981 great changes were in store for the V12 power unit after a £½-million programme to improve fuel economy, long the V12's Achilles heel. Swiss engineer Michael May, from a company called Antipollution Industrial Research, developed a revised cylinder head design (known as the "Fireball") of split level design with two vertical valves in a compact specially machined combustion chamber allowing the use of flat-top pistons. All this meant less weight and lower operating temperatures.

The combustion chamber being on two levels, the inlet valves are lower and closer to the pistons. The exhaust valves are on a higher level. Tangential grooves run from the inlet valve seat to the exhaust so that as the piston nears top dead centre, mixture is squeezed between the piston and inlet valves creating what Jaguar called a "squish". The mixture is swirled around violently, ensuring much more efficient burning. Along with a higher power amplifier, twin coil ignition, a new Lucas digital electronic fuel injection system, a compression ratio raised from 10:1 to 12.5:1, plus a rear axle ratio of 2.88:1, the "new" V12 (to be known as "HE" (for High Efficiency) could deliver around 15mpg on an urban cycle fuel consumption test compared with the old unit's 12mpg, a good 25% improvement. "HE" badges adorned the boots of all V12 models.

There was a number of interior trim changes for 1981. The rear of the centre console was revised to accommodate a cigar lighter on all Daimler models, twin electrically operated door mirrors became standard equipment on Daimlers, and a Daimler logo was featured on the lower section of each front wing similar to the Jaguar emblem on other models. All Daimlers

Daimler Double Six Vanden Plas in Series III form, the most expensive of the range and arguably one of the finest saloons in the world then and now. Headlamp wash/wipe and twin spot lights were standard.

Interior of the Vanden Plas with its own electrically controlled seats, all-hide trim including door trims and console, burr walnut veneers, nylon over-rugs, cruise control, trip computer and air conditioning.

The rear passengers were positively cosseted in the luxury of individually sculptured seats, the centre armrest also forming a cubby.

received the nylon fur rugs in front and rear compartments normally only fitted as standard to Vanden Plas models. Door opening warning lights were now fitted to all doors as standard equipment, with extra warning lights under the front and rear door armrests on Daimlers. A glove box illumination light was now included as standard equipment, activated upon opening the glove box lid. Reading lights were now featured in the rear quarters of the roof panel specifically on Daimlers, activated by moving the light downwards in a swivel mounting. Upper door wood fillets in burr walnut now became standard equipment on all Daimlers as did rear head restraints (optional extra on Jaguars). A new non-reflective black finish to the radio/air conditioning panel replaced the satin finish previously used. The front floor mat incorporated a PVC heel panel now featuring Jaguar or Daimler emblems. Finally, all V12 Daimlers came with the Vanden Plas style chromium-plated body side moulding as standard. It was available as an extra-cost option on other models.

From August 4.2-litre cars had an oil cooler fitted as standard, along with an 18in viscous-coupled cooling fan similar to the V12's one, with thermostatically controlled operation. Improved finish to the bores, identified as "Plateau", was also a new feature on 4.2s from engine no. 8L.99605. All cars (V12s included) were now fitted with new long-life, low-maintenance batteries. A larger clear plastic water header tank was fitted higher up in the engine bay, improving coolant flow. V12s got a revised compression ratio of 10:1 (increased to 12.5:1 for the HE).

In 1981 the exterior colour range was changed again to the following:

> Tudor White
> Indigo Blue
> Damson Red
> Grosvenor Brown
> Sebring Red
> Portland Beige
> Rhodium Silver Metallic
> Cobalt Blue Metallic
> Sapphire Blue Metallic
> Racing Green Metallic
> Chestnut Metallic
> Coronet Gold Metallic
> Garnet Red Metallic
> Sable Metallic
> Biascon Blue Metallic
> Silver Sand Metallic
> Caramel Metallic
> Kingfisher Metallic
> Evergreen Metallic
> Claret Metallic
> Black
> Mineral Blue Metallic

Also available as an extra-cost option was Black Metallic. By this time the new paint processes at Castle Bromwich were in full use, with a vast improvement in finish on all cars.

In December 1981 the battery cooling fan and box were deleted on six-cylinder cars.

In 1982 not much happened on the mechanical side. V12s received revised steering racks with amended lock stop to comply with European regulations, and revised Dunlop D7 tyres of 215 section for better handling. In January Jaguar issued an instruction to dealers concerning difficult gear changes in the five-speed manual transmissions, affecting all Series III and earlier Series II models. It was suggested that to improve the changes the gearbox should be drained and the fluid replaced with Dexron 20 automatic transmission fluid. In the same month all cars received an improved, more accurate electric speedometer.

In February all cars received a new upper steering column to stop extraneous noises, particularly when cornering — effective from Vin no.

336087 (3.4 and 4.2) and 334145 (V12). At Vin no. 334517 childproof locks were fitted to the rear doors, operated by a white plastic knob on the rear door shut face.

In April change came to the automatic transmission quadrant on all models, long a bone of contention because of the detent between D and D2 positions. The detent now took place between D and N, making for easier operation. Whilst the General Motors GM400 automatic transmission remained unaltered on V12 cars, six-cylinder versions received a revised Borg Warner Model 66 unit for smoother changes. The five-speed manual gearbox on six-cylinder models continued unaltered.

With a view to better reliability, standardisation and improved costs Jaguar changed ancillary gauges (fuel, water temperature, oil pressure and battery condition) to the Veglia make from Vin no. 344844, effective on all except Vanden Plas models at this time.

In August 1982 luxury fitments were getting attention on all cars. New GKN silver enamel alloy wheels with two concentric rows of 20 holes (to be known as "Pepperpots") replaced the old style on all Jaguar V12s, and twin electrically operated door mirrors, electric sun roof and revised headlamp wash/wipe system became standard equipment on V12s. For all models front seats received major internal modifications with revised cushion diaphragms to improve comfort and durability. Trim styles were also revised, with discreetly patterned cloth on seat faces for Jaguars, with restyled seat seams. Additional trim padding was featured on the steering wheel, and the interior door handles although still chromium-plated had their surrounds finished in black. To rationalise, the sisal boot floor carpet was reintroduced in PVC-coated felt, with boot side covers in painted hardboard (except for V12s and Daimlers).

Daimler Double Sixes underwent similar treatment but did not get the new alloy wheels as standard, retaining the old "Kent" style. Daimlers lost the chromium-plated bonnet centre strip. Double Six and Vanden Plas seating received unique treatment: not only were the rear seats sculptured as before but detachable rear seat headrests were now standard along with revised fluting on all seats. Deep pile over-rugs were fitted to the rear compartment and the floor carpeting was extended to the base of the "A" posts. Front seats received electric adjustment, previously standard only on Vanden Plas models and still an extra-cost option on Jaguars.

Both 4.2 and V12 Vanden Plas models also came in for extra refinement in 1982, with items including cruise control becoming standard equipment.

On 4.2-litre models trim specification still included tinted windows, quartz halogen headlights, high spec. radio/cassette with electric aerial, lumbar support for the front seats, glove box light, central locking, etc. Daimlers got a new reversible boot mat with rubber on one side and carpet on the other, and rear seat belts became standard equipment.

The list of optional extras was extended (dependent on standard specification) to include electric sunroof, limited slip differential and automatic transmission cruise control.

In August the brake pressure differential warning actuator was deleted from all models, and for the first time all brake pipes were plastic coated.

In October 1982 Jaguar announced that the Daimler name would be dropped from European markets because of its association with Daimler-Benz. The Daimler name was already no longer used in the US market, and many considered that this was a further nail in Daimler's coffin, comments which have since been proved incorrect. Instead of Daimler, a new upmarket model was introduced under the Jaguar banner, badged as the Sovereign (the name previously borne by Daimler XJs anyway). The Sovereign was soon to be destined for the UK market as well, though not replacing the Daimler marque entirely. The Sovereign was in effect a Jaguar-ised version of the Daimler with a similar state of trim.

In November the central locking was rearranged so that it could no longer be operated from the front passenger door lock, the external lock remaining but only working on that door. Thus the central locking could only be operated from the driver's side (from Vin no. 346688). A revised interior rear view mirror was fitted to all models with a stronger coil spring.

At this time Jaguar had introduced a special range of personal accessories to reflect the quality image of their cars, known as the "Jaguar Collection". The range included monogrammed cases, gold key rings, ties, watches, leather wallets, belts, scarfs, etc., all available only from Jaguar dealerships.

For the 1983 model year changes were again made to the interiors, starting with the 3.4s, which received new Raschelle cloth on the seats (standard on this model, a no-cost option on 4.2s and 5.3s). All models now had the same headlining regardless of specification, in a limestone colour. The biggest changes affected the dashboard centre console where the previously satin-finished radio and heating/air conditioning switch panel was now standardised in a more sombre black-grained fabric finish. A new vacuum formed oddments tray was fitted, with auxiliary switch panel incorporating the new clock, lighting rheostat and cigar lighter, but the lower switch panel holding the usual rectangular switches for petrol tank switch-over, etc., remained. Both panels were now finished in wood veneer, burr walnut on Daimlers and Sovereigns, walnut on others. Jaguar had developed a process for veneering directly on to metal, as Rolls-Royce had done on the Camargue.

On those models fitted with a trip computer this was positioned in the upper panel, allowing space in the centre of the lower panel (previously used for the standard analogue clock) to feature a scripted "Jaguar" or "Daimler" badge. Because the new console arrangement took up slightly more depth the automatic transmission quadrant was moved aft for greater clearance. Finally, a thicker rimmed steering wheel with altered horn push arrived on Daimler models, and the graphics on the lights switch were changed on all models.

The on-board computer should have special mention as it brought the XJ range well and truly into the electronics era. Although many consider such equipment a gimmick it is fair to say that the on-board computer system can be very useful to the driver. It indicates:

Amount of fuel held in the tanks.

Fuel consumption at any moment in time (updated every 15 seconds).

Distance travelled on a journey, since filling up with fuel, etc.

Average speed of the vehicle on a journey or other period.

Time and time expired.

It can be switched off when not needed, can simply be re-set, and can be instructed to convert mph to kmh. In all it is a complex but comprehensive system, extremely easy to use and with the added facility of "holding" its information indefinitely (providing the battery of the vehicle is not disconnected). Although the system to some extent eliminates the need for a mileage trip meter and fuel gauge, the conventional types are still retained on the dashboard. On Daimler and Vanden Plas models and Sovereigns the trip computer became a standard fitment.

Externally, minor changes were made to all models. The 3.4s at last were equipped with a single coachline along the sides and quartz halogen headlights were fitted. All Daimlers now featured a chromium-plated side moulding but the centre bonnet strip was discontinued, which meant slight alterations to the Daimler grille. All cars received new front wing mounted leaping cat badges and the silver-on-black Jaguar radiator badge, previously on six-cylinder cars was standardised for V12s as well.

Revised style stainless steel wheel trims incorporating a detachable stainless hub cap were fitted to higher specification models, looking a lot "cleaner" than the old style with exposed wheel nuts. The wheel trim itself was still retained by the wheel nuts (underneath the hub caps).

Exterior colour schemes were amended again and to rationalise were reduced to fiteen colours. Colours deleted at this time were:

Damson Red
Garnet
Mineral Blue
Caramel
Kingfisher
Evergreen

In January 1983 Jaguar issued a written warning to all dealers concering the fitment of wire wheels to XJ saloons, particularly aiming their comments at a type known as Zenith which had specifically caused problems. It was emphasised again (as it had been many years before in connection with Series I XJs) that conventional wire wheels were unsuitable due to wheel loadings under heavy cornering conditions.

In April, due to complaints on 1982 and prior models of premature front seat sagging, dealers were asked to supplement the foam filler to boost seat shaping. In the same month, due to supply problems, the Phillips GCA-637 radio/cassette unit was superseded by the Phillips AC420 unit. At that time the crankshaft oil thrower was reinstated on six-cylinder engines to overcome leakage of oil past the oil seal, effective from engines 8L. 136128 (4.2) and 8A.14120 (3.4). A new cloth trim made of woven velour instead of polyester was used for non-leather trim models. The colours were:

Graphite
Fleet Blue
Beige
Amber

In June six-cylinder engines received revised camshaft covers with additional internal ribbing to give more strength. This allowed the torque figures to be increased when tightening the chromium-plated dome nuts to 7.8lb/ft. (not recommended for earlier covers).

In September further sound system changes took place with the replacement of Phillips by a higher quality Clarion system, PU-7009A, for all models except Vanden Plas, this model receiving the PU-9021A system. Due to complaints of groans from the power steering under high speed cornering, Jaguar introduced new pinion housing seals supplied by Shamban. Responding to complaints of body creaks Jaguar found that foam padding between the fume baffle and rear inner wings could get dislodged, and that incorrect welding of the overlap joint above the rear parcel shelf caused a creak in the D post around the rear screen aperture, further emphasised in some cases by insecure fitting of the screen itself.

For the 1984 model year the Jaguar Sovereign was finally released on the home market with all the Daimler extras including rear reading lights, over-rugs, air conditioning, sculptured stainless steel wheel trims and carpeted boot (although not including, surprisingly, the Daimler style individual rear seats). The all-in no-extras price of around £18,500 for a 4.2-litre version was some £2,500 more than a normal 4.2-litre Jaguar but £1,000 less than the Vanden Plas version still available. The V12 version known as the Sovereign HE had everything the 4.2-litre had plus headlamp wash/wipe, cruise control, electrically operated sun roof, on-board computer and a high specification radio/cassette system. The alloy "pepperpot" wheels were even at this late stage still an extra-cost option. The all-in price of the

The Jaguar Sovereign, here seen in 4.2-litre form, became the top model in the Jaguar range, offering similar accommodation to the Daimler but without the individually sculptured seats.

Sovereign HE was a cool £21,000. In the previous three years the prices of the 3.4 and 4.2 "standard" cars had remained virtually static, making them exceptional value at £14,000 for a 3.4 and £16,000 for a 4.2. Only two Daimlers remained in the range, the 4.2 at £23,000 and the Double Six at £27,000, both with the usual high specification including fog/spot lights, electric sun roof, wood fillets and the old style alloy wheels. The HE badge was for some reason dropped from the Double Six badging on the boot at this time.

The range of exterior colour schemes was again revised to:

Tudor White
Black
Grosvenor Brown
Rhodium Silver Metallic
Cobalt Blue Metallic
Sapphire Blue Metallic
Racing Green Metallic
Coronet Gold Metallic
Claret
Silver Sand Metallic
Clarendon Blue
Sirrus
Cranberry
Antelope
Sage Green
Regent Grey

With the demise of the Vanden Plas model the Double Six took up the role of flagship, offering virtually the same accommodation and trim level

In January 1984, after many complaints of water leaking into the car, Jaguar found a lack of sealant to the drip channels, A, B and C post seals and faults in the front windscreen pillar sealing.

By April Jaguar had listed as available for the first time complete matching wood veneer kits in case of damage; it had been found impossible to match existing veneers and colours.

In July new Kienzle door mirror motors were fitted to improve reliability. At the same time an improved electric motor was fitted for the radio aerial.

After reports of excessive oil consumption on 4.2-litre cars new piston ring packs were made availabe. To overcome sticking valves new exhaust valve guides were recommended, involving relieving the valve guide bore at the exhaust port end from engine nos. 8L.167200 (4.2) and 8A.15507 (3.4).

In September all six-cylinder engines received a Sursulpha hardened crankshaft from engine nos. 8L.168437 (4.2) and 8A.15562 (3.4).

In November a revised Clarion model E.950 hi-fi radio/cassette deck with dual-intensity lighting became available as standard equipment on Sovereigns and Daimlers, optional for other models.

For the 1985 model year changes were still coming fast and furious, for in March a revised trip computer with CMOS technology was fitted (interchangeable with previous models) incorporating Watchdog circuitry to prevent what Jaguar termed as "wipe-out" problems. It had been noted that power surge could cause the computer to lose its held information on journey times, consumption, etc. The new computer also incorporated the facility to run the mileometer to 999.9 miles.

A new power steering rack without the rack damper grease nipple and with a new tangential valve and torsion bar was used from Vin no. 413000, this being brought about mainly because the use of wrong lubricants had caused damage to racks with grease nipples.

Complaints had been received of alloy wheels sticking to the hub spigots due to corrosion between the surfaces. All cars from this time had hubs and wheels greased with Shell Retinax A grease.

On 4.2-litre cars the air conditioning receiver/dryer was moved to ensure the maximum refrigerant flow, the sight glass now on the left in a vertical position; because of underbonnet space restrictions V12 cars remained unchanged. 4.2s also received a new Ducellier coil, ballast resistor, modified amplifier and harness to improve ignition performance, from engine no. 8L.173271.

Under severe weather conditions causing the radio aerial to freeeze in the erected position, it was noted that attempts to retract the mast could blow a fuse causing the door-open warning lights to stay on. A diode was fitted in the system to safeguard the circuitry on all subsequent models and was fitted to existing cars by dealers.

In July an improved thermo-plastic acrylic paint system was adopted.

In September an entirely new electric central locking system was introduced incorporating full electric motor operation for doors and boot instead of the previous electro-solenoid system. This became effective from Vin nos. 428715 (lhd) and 429455 (rhd).

In November, due to problems with corroded wheel nuts on the pepperpot alloy wheels, Jaguar replaced these with stainless steel nuts.

For 1986 and beyond improvements were still to be made to the Series III cars. Despite the age of the original design, Jaguar's continued programme of improvement in both quality control and reliability had helped to keep the XJs in very heavy demand, particularly fortunate for Jaguar as the new XJ40 was still not ready for release.

The interior came in for more changes. For the 3.4-litre cars a new herringbone pattern wool-tweed upholstery was standardised (which could also be ordered for high spec. models at no extra cost). All models including the 3.4 received new walnut trim to the top of the centre console and around the gearlever housing. Veneered door fillets arrived on 3.4s and 4.2s, previously fitted only on the higher-priced models. Stainless steel sill kick-plates featuring the "Jaguar" or "Daimler" name were now fitted on all models along with rear seat belts, electric door mirrors and tinted glass. Revised chromium-plated surrounds were fitted to door handles, radio system and front seat adjusters. Badging was altered yet again: this time the "HE" and all litre markings were dropped. Instead of the previous plastic scripted badges, chromium-plated rectangular badges with the names embossed in black were now used. Some new colours arrived: Curlew Brown, Windsor Blue and Steel Blue.

For the North American market, only two models were now available: the XJ6 and the Vanden Plas (under the Jaguar name).

In July 1986 a revised Mark 3 air conditioning system with computer controlled module was fitted on Series III saloons. The temperature control switch now had a manual override and an entirely new protection clutch system for the compressor was used. This system was a considerable improvement and is still used on Series III V12s.

Revised interior of the 3.4-litre XJ6, with new wool-blend tweed upholstery and plain wood veneer on the centre console.

In August, after constant complaints about the sunroof, which when fully open caused severe buffeting inside the car (the factory had previously issued a suggestion that the sunroof should not be opened the last 1½-2in) Jaguar developed a sunroof deflector produced in tinted acrylic with a discreet Jaguar logo. Fitted to the roof at the front of the sunroof aperture the deflector (still an extra-cost option, part no. JLM.9831) had the desired effect.

From V12 engine no. 7P.55762, spark plug leads were altered, with a new angle on leads 1A and 1B to improve fitment and accessibility.

May 1987 saw the last XJ6 Series III leave the Browns Lane factory. (The very last right hand drive car is still in the hands of Jaguar today as a memorial to the XJ models.) This marked the demise of the famous XK six-cylinder engine in a passenger vehicle application (other than the DS420 limousine) although at the time of writing a heavily modified version of the engine is still in military use. The V12 has remained in production and has continued to be developed to this day.

In May 1988 the exterior colour Glacier White was reformulated to give improved opacity. In October Crimson (a recent addition to the range) was also reformulated after unfortunate reactions in hot conditions.

In March 1989 a recalibration of the GM400 automatic transmission unit took place to improve responsiveness, particularly on kickdown:

Change Speeds	Full Throttle		Kickdown	
Gear changes	1 to 2	2 to 3	3 to 2	3 to 1
Mph	53/60	94/99	96/108	44/50

May of that year, at Vin. no. 481680, V12 engines were adapted to take 95 octane unleaded fuel. At this time appropriate labels were fitted to most production cars to that effect. A new one-piece rear main bearing oil seal replaced the previous rope type from engine no. 7P.02073, along with a new single solid state ignition coil.

In October, Jaguar eliminated the need to grease the hubs at 15,000-mile intervals, effective from Vin no. 482000.

In November, due to complaints of air pump noises from resonances in the air cleaner covers, Jaguar recommended existing cars have a 19mm hole drilled in the cover opposite the air pump pick-up port in the backplate.

For the 1990 model year Jaguar finally brought the V12 Series III cars into line with all other Jaguars with the introduction of ABS anti-lock braking. A revised steering wheel and the extra-cost option of an auto-changer CD player situated in the boot also helped the Series IIIs to soldier on for the remainder of their lives.

Colour combinations available in 1990/91 were:

Solid Colours
Black
Glacier White
Grenadier Red
Jaguar Racing Green
Westminster Blue

Metallic Colours
Talisman Silver
Tungsten
Savoy Grey
Diamond Blue
Arctic Blue
Solent Blue
Satin Beige
Bordeaux Red

Special Option Micatallic Colours
Jade Green
Gunmetal
Regency Red

Leather trim
Magnolia
Doeskin
Barley
Parchment
Savile Grey
Isis Blue
Mulberry
Charcoal

Special leather trim with contrasting piping
Savile Grey with mid grey, isis blue or mulberry piping.
Doeskin with isis blue or mulberry piping.
Magnolia with isis blue or mulberry piping.
Parchment with sage green piping.

The very last Jaguar V12 Sovereign left the factory in November 1991, destined to stay in Jaguar's Heritage Collection alongside its sister XJ6 of 1986. The Daimler Double Six carries on in very limited production using up body shells until the introduction of its successor. There is no doubt that

The current Jaguar Sovereign and Daimler Double Six, now with A.B.S. braking as standard equipment.

the V12 Series III still has a very solid and enthusiastic following. At the time of writing only a few cars are produced per month at Jaguar, making the V12 very exclusive, but all production is eagerly taken up and the car is reaching new heights of acclaim in such unforeseen markets as Japan, as the future "classic" of the Jaguar/Daimler marque. Outclassed it may be in terms of sophistication when compared with the latest offerings in the XJ40, but there is no doubt in my mind that the V12 Series III is still a car to be reckoned with and a classic in its own time.

ABOVE. Sovereign V12 badging, 1990.

RIGHT & BELOW. Interior of the 1990 Sovereign V12, showing new style steering wheel and contrasting piping on the seats.

What the Press said

The Series III saloon received a wider range of road tests than any other version of the XJ, and the first to evaluate the new model was *Autocar* in March 1979 under the heading "Perfecting the near-perfect? . . . well, Browns Lane try to". Noting a price increase of between 8 and 11% pro rata on the old Series II models, *Autocar* welcomed many of the revised driver comforts, generally finding the new models unspoilt and better than before.

In July 1979 *What Car* published a comparative test between the Series III XJ12, BMW 730 and Mercedes-Benz 280SE. Against the Jaguar was its awful fuel consumption — under 11mpg compared to the manual-transmission BMW at over 17 and the Mercedes at just under 14. Coupled to this was the noted complexity of the V12 engine bay, but the writers were in no doubt about the Jaguar's extraordinary smoothness and its exhilarating performance. The Jaguar also scored on its splendid wood and leather interior compared with the very bland offerings from Germany.

On levels of equipment the Jaguar won hands down, with many items like electric windows, radio, etc. as standard equipment whereas all this was extra on both the German cars. The Jaguar was the dearest car to run (because of fuel consumption) and to buy out of the three, at £15,766 compared to the Mercedes at £13,578 and the BMW at £12,399; however, on servicing and spares costs the Jaguar was much the cheapest to maintain.

Performance was also in the Jaguar's favour, with a 0-60mph time of 8 seconds compared to 8.6 (manual BMW) and 9.4 (Mercedes) and 0-100mph in a stunning 17.9 seconds compared to 25.4 and 25.5 respectively!

After their initial evaluation *Autocar* carried out a full test on a 4.2-litre XJ6 Series III saloon in December 1979, noting dramatically better performance than from the Series II and much improved economy. In *Autocar's* eyes the Jaguar was one of the jewels of the British motor industry. They compared the Jaguar with the larger-engined Mercedes 450 SEL (£5,000 dearer, 7mph faster, 2mpg thirstier) the BMW 732 (same price as the Jaguar, same top speed, better acceleration and fuel economy) and three cars trying hard to but never quite matching the prestige of the other three, the Ford Granada, Opel Senator and Peugeot 604, all much cheaper but in other terms no match for the Jaguar.

In contrast *Wheels* magazine in 1980 carried out a "Battle Royal" between the V12 Jaguar and the Mercedes 450 SE (a much fairer match with the V12 than with the XJ6). They were aiming to find the best saloon in the world and found it a difficult task in view of the two cars' vastly differing style and appeal, coming to no final conclusion other than to award both cars the accolade. The Mercedes scored on finish, fuel consumption, refinement of equipment, build quality and mileage between services. The Jaguar's handling was superb and the overall feel of the British prestige car could not be matched by the Mercedes.

After a 12,000-mile long-term assessment in 1980 *Autocar* came to the conclusion that the XJ6 was "The Coventry-made marvel . . . in a car like this, the faults hardly matter!" During the test the very fully equipped Jaguar (air conditioning, cruise control, remote control door mirrors, electric driver's seat, headlamp wash/wipe and stereo radio/cassette) suffered only minor faults, starting with the electric aerial not erecting fully, stretched drive belts, a leaking wheel bearing oil seal and, by the end of the period, a slight whine from the rear axle. Other faults included a central locking fault in the nearside front door, an annoying noise from the air conditioning system and a cracked water reservoir filler cap. Wind noise caused some problems (echoed by many owners at the time) and the paint started to chip in not-so-usual places, confirming many reports of poor quality preparation at the factory.

In 1982 *Motor* took to the roads in a new Daimler Double Six HE (with the Fireball head), finding the car much improved in terms of economy and arguably the British motor industry's finest achievement at that time. Fuel consumption had improved to a touring figure of 15.6mpg with no loss in overall performance. At £20,000 the Daimler was exceptionally well equipped, though the testers thought that air conditioning and a better quality radio/cassette system should have been included in the price. They clearly identified the Daimler as a better quality vehicle than other Jaguar/Daimler XJs previously tested.

Motor briefly compared the Daimler to the Audi 200T, BMW 735i and Opel Senator, all cheaper than the Daimler, the Mercedes 380 SEL (same price as the Daimler) and the Aston Martin Lagonda at two and a half times the price! Only the expensive Lagonda could match the top speed of the Daimler.

Modern Motor tested a Jaguar 4.2 XJ6 with manual gearbox declaring it "A gutsy big six, plus one of the best rolling chassis in the world, a self-indulgent winner when it has the five-speed manual gearbox!" They found the Jaguar a real driver's car but with plenty of sophistication, scoring maximum five star ratings on comfort and brakes, four stars on handling, performance and quietness, and dropping to three stars on finish, luggage capacity and value for money.

Even as late as 1985 the XJ in V12 form was still in among the winners when *Car* announced its Top Ten of the year. Among such esteemed cars as the Ferrari 308GTB, Porsche 911, Range Rover, Mercedes 500 SEL and Golf GTi, the Jaguar delivered 140mph with smoothness and silence that no other car could match, and provided the best compromise of refinement with handling.

XJ Miscellany

It is a useful exercise at this point to review the various models from the owner/driver's point of view. In this chapter we will also look at some different types of XJ, from the bizarre to the unusual, from kit car to cabriolet.

Police XJs

We can start with perhaps one of the most frequent yet daunting sights on our roads — the Police Jaguar. Jaguars have been regular transport for our Police forces for years, from the early days of the SS in the thirties, but perhaps the two models most commonly associated with the force have been the Mark II in the sixties and the XJ in the seventies and eighties.

Jaguar were issuing 4.2-litre XJs to Police forces from as early as 1969 but it wasn't until the introduction of the Series II in the mid-seventies that the company made any specific moves to target this lucrative and prestigious market. With the Series II came the "PS" (Police Specification) model, manufactured with the Police forces in mind. Nearly always 4.2-litre versions, these were adapted during production to meet the various criteria

Police Specification Series
I XJ6.

Series II XJ6 PS model in the familiar 'jam sandwich' scheme.

demanded, which included high mileage and 18-hour working days. Cloth or Ambla trim replaced the leather, rubber matting replaced the tufted carpets, and black matt vinyl the polished veneer. High-lift camshafts and in some cases suspension modifications, close ratio gearboxes, high axle ratios, heavy duty ancillary equipment and even a special Police White exterior colour scheme could be specified.

Unfortunately the Series IIs were up against stiff competition for Police business from the stalwart Ford Granadas and even more so from the ultra-reliable BMW 5 series cars. Jaguar was losing ground, that is until the introduction of the Series III, when Coventry started to fight back. Whilst early examples of Series III cars were not that well built or reliable Jaguar were getting a better image but at that time still seemed hampered by high running costs when compared with the competition. However, since the early eighties XJ saloons have been used by over twenty forces in the country.

At the time of writing most forces were in the process of changing Series IIIs for XJ40s but I was fortunate to make contact with my local force, the South Yorkshire Police Traffic Division, who had two Series III cars, supplied new in 1986 but just coming up for replacement (by new Jaguars). PC Pete Thompson was most helpful in providing some background to the cars. Both were purchased in unmarked Police White livery (without stripes) and finished to Police Specification. The main differences are an improved fuel injection system for the standard 4.2-litre engine, high-lift camshafts, stiffened and slightly lowered suspension and a beefed-up five-speed manual gearbox. Due to extra electrical loading the Jaguars were equipped with uprated systems including heavy duty battery and alternator. Externally, apart from the white paint finish, the PS badging and the three aerials, the cars were standard Jaguar even down to tyre specification and exterior trim level.

Internally, the cars were very different, with black rubber matting replacing carpeting, black/grey woven upholstery and plain black vinyl door panels, the latter with austere handles and door pulls (although speaker grilles were still accommodated — for Police radio use rather than stereophonic sound). Most of the veneered woodwork was replaced by simple black vinyl although some wood remained on the standard dash panel. The glove compartment was replaced by Vascar speed control equipment, with recalibrated speedometer for the observer matching the standard (although recalibrated) dash-mounted speedometer. On the centre console were the standard heating controls plus special switching for the various warning lights, hazard lights, horns, etc., as well as the standard equipment Police telephone. Electric windows were standard. In the boot plain matting was fitted, with no sound-deadening on the boot lid or for that matter the bonnet.

The two South Yorkshire PS XJ6s, now to be replaced by more modern XJ40 versions.

Dashboard arrangement of a typical PS XJ6 with some wood veneer retained. Note the glove box lid featuring Vascar radar equipment and the switchgear on the centre console.

At first the cars were used in "plain clothes" form for shows, Royal convoys, etc., and were subsequently fitted with fluorescent striping as the current photographs show. While under test by PC Thompson and his partners, the Jaguars were found to be fitted with incorrect rear axle ratios giving a maximum speed of only around 105mph which, of course, was totally unsuitable, particularly for motorway work. This was a common failing on the Police Specification cars as many others were altered before entering service. Revised differentials were fitted by the factory and the cars were returned for further assessment. Under test conditions, without roof mounted warning lights, etc., one of the cars attained a maximum speed of 142mph.

Both cars have naturally had a hard life, one having completed 160,000 miles and the other 183,000 miles at the time of writing. They have been reliable although both cars have had "blown" engines in their time. One must bear in mind that they are put under extremely strenuous loads when compared with our own everyday cars; for example it is not unusual at the scene of an accident on a motorway for a Police patrol car to remain at rest with the engine at idle for a couple of hours keeping the battery charged against the load of hazard lights, headlights, etc.

Police officers have found the Jaguars a joy to drive and Pete Thompson commented that the cars command a degree of respect from the motorist on the motorway, far more so than the Ford Granadas and Rover 827s in the current South Yorkshire fleet.

Problems common to both cars have been condensation and poor ventilation, the heating system being inadequate for continuous driving and standing work — not a patch on a Ford! The Rovers are faster than the Jaguars but then the Jags have had a hard life and have covered higher mileages. Shortly to be replaced by XJ40s, these Series IIIs will long be remembered by the officers who have regularly driven them. After a programme of "privatisation" including removing stripes, electrical equipment and signing, these Jaguars are destined for the auction room at knockdown prices. One day perhaps someone will "restore" a Police Specification XJ6 for posterity!

Whilst talking of Police Jaguars, we should also make mention of the many other Jaguars in our Police forces today, particularly the regular transport of our Chief Constables; unmarked standard specification models, usually finished in black, green, blue or white, have been and still are used, from 4.2s to V12 Sovereigns. Apart from the radio aerial these cars are usually nondescript although many have specially adapted blue flashing lights fixed behind the radiator grille or underneath the front bumper.

Official cars

Perhaps the best-known XJ is used by the Prime Minister. The official Prime Ministerial Daimler Double Six is one of a fleet of XJs, both Daimlers and Jaguars, supplied for official use with varying degrees of specification dependent on the status of the Minister or department. After a period of Rootes domination, with Pullmans, Imperials and Super Snipes, through the

Rover era, with 3 litres and today 820s, Jaguar is now well established on the "official" scene. Full details of the Prime Minister's car are not openly available; suffice to say that the car is to full Double Six trim specification with some hidden extras. For example the body panels are reinforced with bullet-proof materials, and because of the use of bullet-proof glass throughout the car no window winder mechanisms are fitted, the glass being too thick and heavy. The window frames are reinforced accordingly. As there are no opening windows, an uprated air conditioning system is provided. A special telephone system is included in the specification as are revised (larger and bullet-proof) rear head restraints. All this work is carried out so discreetly that the car looks quite normal. Unfortunately, the V12 will shortly be retiring in favour of a new Daimler from the XJ40 stable.

Many of our Royal family patronise Jaguar and Daimler, and the Royal fleet presently includes a V12 Sovereign and a Double Six. In some cases members of the Royal household on visits around the country have been known to contact local dealers to "borrow" a V12 for the occasion!

Cabriolets, conversions and one-offs

One of the most unusual XJs ever produced was a special cabriolet based around a 2.8-litre de luxe automatic saloon. The car was converted to four-door cabriolet form by a local company in Mauritius for the Royal Tour of that area and the Falklands in 1972. The car was not new at the time and remained a four-door with window frames. It had little extra bracing save for a thin "T" bar across the car between the B/C posts. Little else is known of the car, which if not further structurally reinforced is unlikely to have survived.

The XJ6 2.8-litre cabriolet prepared for the Queen's visit to Mauritius. Note the lack of support for the window frames.

At the 1984 Motor Show an unusual "stretched" V12 Series III saloon turned up. The car, designed and built by RS Panels of Nuneaton, was (and still is) the only 12-cylinder limousine available and provided an interesting alternative to the "stretched" Americans or even Daimler's own DS420 limousines. It was intended to be available in both Jaguar and Daimler forms, with overall length increased by 32in and height by 4in. Particular attention was paid to structural rigidity and quality of finish. As an indication of the skill with which the conversion was executed, there was no vinyl roof covering to hide the welded joins in the panels. Although standard XJ doors were used these were obviously heavily modified and special double underbody sills were incorporated to improve rigidity. The Motor Show car was finished in claret with optional extras such as cocktail cabinet (with electric doors) and separate rear compartment air conditioning. TWR Speedlite alloy wheels were also featured. With improved front and rear seating, the limousine also had foldaway occasional seats adapted from the DS420 limousine. It is not known how many of these cars were produced.

Brothers Dominic and Dale Chappelle own a most unusual Series III Daimler Sovereign 4.2 "V" registered four-door cabriolet. The Chappelles were looking for a prestige car, but something a little unusual, and a local motor dealer found them this cabriolet. Originally converted by Cabriolets International of Poulton Le Fylde near Blackpool in Lancashire, this car has also undergone a respray in cobalt blue with colour-coding to bumpers, sill styling kit and pepperpot alloy wheels. Interestingly, the existing doors, side windows, rear bodywork, rain gutters and 2-3in of roof section at the sides remain intact, helping to maximise the stiffness of the structure without the roof. A targa bar, strategically mounted at the B and C posts, stretches across the width of the car, just as on the earlier Mauritius car but of more substantial size. The hood does not drop into a recess but sits on the parcel shelf behind the rear seat. Lowering it involves unclipping two windscreen clamps and manually folding it backwards. A tonneau cover is provided which clips into position completely covering the lowered hood and giving some degree of protection to rear seat passengers from back-draughts. It is not, unfortunately, possible to position the hood in the midway position, sedanca style. With the hood up the roof line is very similar to that of a standard saloon and from the side (at a distance) the hood could be mistaken for a vinyl roof covering. A large perspex rear window allows ample rearward vision.

On the road the car is still very taut, but some degree of shake can be felt over poor roads. With the hood erect wind noise is low, aided by Velcro strips at the edges where the hood meets the roof sections. On this particular car the hood is not lined although I understand that on the latest conversions a nylon lining is fitted.

The Cabriolets International conversion represented a very attractive, unusual but practical way of converting a standard XJ saloon into something a little special at a realistic price. Unfortunately the company is no longer trading.

Cabriolet
International-prepared
XJ6 makes a very effective
convertible.

Neat roofline of the
Cabriolet International
conversion.

For those wishing to produce an XJ convertible the Coupé was the ideal basis. Although Jaguar themselves were never officially involved, other companies took up the challenge, perhaps the best-known and most effective conversion being by Ladbroke Avon Limited of Warwick. They made a relatively large number of convertible Coupés (both six- and twelve-cylinder) with a superbly designed hood and hood mechanism. The cars were suitably strengthened underneath and many survive today as testimony to the development work carried out to make the cars practical, safe and long-lived. Some cars were updated to Series III specification with the adoption of rubber bumpers and other items of external trim.

There have been some abortive attempts at producing convertibles based on four-door cars, but I am not aware of any that survive.

Others have attempted to convert Coupés but many such cars have not undergone sufficient strengthening work to make them safe — removing the roof from any car is a task that should be undertaken with the greatest care to ensure the rigidity of the body structure, particularly with a car such as the XJ, which has no separate chassis. Perhaps now, with the increasing value of the Coupé models, there will be less activity in this area. After all, if Sir

ABOVE. Example of the Avon Stevens convertible, based on a two door Coupé.

Another XJC convertible.

The only known Series III convertible retaining front doors from a four-door saloon.

William Lyons had intended there to be an XJ Convertible, would he not have produced one himself?

Ladbroke Avon also produced the Jaguar XJ Estate Car in the early eighties. This represented a top-quality utility vehicle at a time when only Mercedes and Reliant were offering anything similar. The top of the bodywork from the "B" post backwards was cut off and replaced by a revised straight-through roof and a one-piece top-hinged tailgate. The roof was vinyl-covered and special rear side windows were fitted, but the rest of the exterior remained unchanged.

Ladbrokes managed very successfully to graft their bodywork on to the existing Jaguar styling, retaining the shape of the rear windows, rear valance and even the light clusters and lower section of the boot lid, the upper part of the tail gate being taken from a Renault 5 but looking quite natural on the XJ! Perhaps the only negative factors in the design are the fuel filler caps high up in the rear quarters and the slightly hearse-like appearance from behind.

A lot of attention was paid to detail in the interior, with matching leather and good quality carpet trim, although because of the intrusion of the fuel tanks in each rear wing a good 6in of space on either side was lost to the boxed-in tanks. The rear seat back was, as usual in an estate car, more upright, and it only folded on to the fixed rear seat cushion.

The car was revealed to the public at the 1980 Birmingham Motor Show, where is took a Gold Medal for coachwork. At a price of £6,500 (plus the cost of the car, of course) the conversion was not cheap, but it was after all hand built. An optional extra was extra child seats, facing rearwards and folding flat below the rear loading floor (à la Mercedes and Peugeot), for a cost of £475.

There have been many other attempts at conversions of XJs, particularly for such purposes as custom cars and, ironically, pick-ups (could Jaguar have found a market for an XJ Ute in Australia?) Many have found it relatively easy to convert an old XJ into a pick-up and some examples are illustrated here. Always (to date!) involving Series I or II cars, some are quite basic, others well executed with looks enhanced by the use of Coupé roof panels. Just how many of these cars exist is not known, although a good example of a six-wheeled pick-up is still (at the time of writing) in the Nottingham area.

The Avon Stevens XJ6 estate.

XJ6 pick-up, based on a
Series II saloon, with
Coupé roof panels.

A V12 Series I pick-up
with 'woody' rear end and
truck exhaust pipes.

Jaguar factory records contain information on a number of other interesting vehicles, some still around today, some destroyed and others whose whereabouts are not known. One example is Sir Williams Lyons' own XJ, a 4.2-litre Series I appropriately registered PHP 42G. This car (chassis no. IL. 1370) is now fortunately kept in Jaguar's own collection of historic vehicles and is quite often on show at the Browns Lane factory.

Two early Series I XJs were fitted with experimental V8 engines of 3,565cc, registered PKV 666G (chassis no. IL.2079) and RRW 513H (chassis no. IL.3777). These engines were later abandoned due to lack of smoothness and cost of future development but nothing is known of the fate of the two cars.

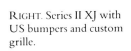

RIGHT. Series II XJ with US bumpers and custom grille.

A rather unusual short XJ6.

Customised XJ with picnic table spoiler.

Widened wheel arches with air scoops to aid brake cooling.

RHP 899H was an XJ6 adapted to take a V12 prototype engine, built for and driven by Sir William Lyons and later Bob Knight. This car, which pre-dates the V12 E Type by two years and the production XJ12 by three years, incorporated unusual features including a rear view mirror with direction indicator repeaters, apparently designed by Sir William himself, an oil temperature gauge on the dashboard, and a Phillips stereo cassette recorder incorporating a separate microphone for dictation, ordered specifically by Sir William. Finished in sable with cinnamon interior, the rest of the car was pure XJ6. This historically important car has survived in the hands of John Peters and is currently undergoing total restoration.

Chassis no. IL.2927 (registration no. RHP 133H), another car originally used as a test bed for the V12 engine back in 1969/70, was called off the production line by Sir William and later used by Lofty England. This car was later converted to full V12 Series I specification and eventually passed on to Silverstone Racing Circuit for use as a high speed fire tender, with suitable modifications to carry fire fighting equipment. Repainted in red and yellow with appropriate signing and blue lights, the car was to be seen at Silverstone for many years until pensioned off, and is now exhibited in the Coventry Motor Museum. It was replaced at Silverstone by an XJ40, again supplied by Jaguar.

The Silverstone Fire Tender adapted from experimental XJ12 Series I donated by Jaguar Cars.

Also to be seen at race tracks but better known for its involvement in the Thrust II World Land Speed Record attempt was a Series III XJ12 similarly adapted as a fire tender. On loan to the Richard Noble record breaking team, this particular car saw dramatic work in the desert and on salt flats preparing the ground for Thrust II before the record attempts. At speeds of up to 135mph for 12-hour stretches the Jaguar behaved impeccably.

In 1975 a Series II XJ12L saloon was converted to accept an adapted 6.4-litre version of the engine along with a five-speed gearbox to assess durability. Registered HRW 75N (chassis no. 2R.3757), this car was used extensively by Harold Mundy but appears to have been eventually scrapped.

In 1978 the last production XJ 5.3C (chassis no. 2G.1604) was assigned to the Heritage collection of vehicles. Since that time the last of the 4.2-litre XJ Jaguar Sovereigns has also been retained. At the time of writing, as the V12 Sovereign/Double Six is still in production there are no plans to retain one of these; however, in view of the lengthy production run and the enormous success of the Series III perhaps Jaguar ought to consider saving one for posterity.

Before leaving the topic of unusual and special XJs we must make mention of a very special XJ V12 Coupé prepared as a replica (in most ways) of the Broadspeed XJ Coupés. The car in question, finished in British Racing Green with tan leather interior, was prepared specially for *The New Avengers* TV series for the personal use of John Steed. The idea of such a Jaguar came from the fact that Steed in his previous series had used a vintage Bentley, and although he used a Rover 3500 SD1, it was thought his character demanded something unusual and distinctly personal for his transport — enter the XJ Coupé. Whilst the car had many of the racing Coupé modifications, including wide alloy wheels, lowered suspension and uprated engine, its handling was unsatisfactory and the car could become positively unsafe at speed. After being used in the series, it progressed to various promotional exhibitions and was, I understand, sold at a later date, only to be written off.

XJ-based replicas

It is worth taking a look at some of the replica vehicles built around XJ mechanicals. The most noteworthy range of cars from the seventies was built by the Panther Westwinds company in Surrey. Two models were produced, the J72 sports car and the DeVille luxury saloon/convertible.

The J72 was introduced in 1972, offering a passing similarity to the pre-war SS100 Jaguar sports car although not pretending to be a true replica of that fine vehicle. Initially supplied with a 3.8-litre Mark II saloon engine, most

The Panther J72 replica SS based around XJ6 mechanics.

The Panther DeVille, styled loosely after a Bugatti Royale and based on XJ6 or V12 mechanics.

production cars had a 4.2-litre XJ saloon power unit driving through an XJ all-synchromesh gearbox with overdrive. A sturdy handbuilt tubular chassis was designed to take XJ suspension, disc brakes and even XJ wheels and tyres (although most cars ended up equipped with wire wheels). Many items of Jaguar trim were also used. Options could include automatic transmission, air-conditioning, power-assisted steering and even a detachable aluminium hard top. By 1973 the J72 was also offered with the Jaguar XJ V12 power unit and transmission including Powr-Lok limited slip differential.

The other model from the Panther stable was the extravagant DeVille, available in saloon or convertible form. The DeVille's styling was also 1930s-inspired, this time drawing on the Bugatti Royale not only in looks but also in sheer size and stature: 17ft long, 5ft 1in high and 5ft 11in wide. Offering limousine comfort as well as proportions these cars were meant to be outrageous, for the man who wanted to be noticed, for rich Arabian princes, for film stars or simply for the extrovert! With a kerb weight of 4,368lb, the DeVille had everything or anything the owner desired: an endless range of exterior and interior colour schemes, air conditioning, electric windows, electric sliding roof and maybe even telephone, television, cocktail bar, and so on. Although hand-built in aluminium the DeVille had Austin 1800 doors and some trim from other models. Internally very high quality hides and Wilton carpets were used, along with many XJ-sourced trim items. Mechanically the DeVille normally featured XJ V12 mechanics but a few were produced with 4.2-litre XJ power units. The convertible version is even rarer than the saloon. It had only two doors, pillarless windows and a fully trimmed Everflex detachable hardtop in addition to the mohair soft top.

A more recent XJ-based vehicle is the Aristocat, designed and built as a replica of the XK120 sports car in Lancashire by Anthony Taylor. In production for several years now the kit (most are supplied in kit form to be built up by owners) is very well designed and executed, founded on a spaceframe chassis, painted in red oxide or galvanised, which will take the majority of XJ mechanics (even a V12 engine if desired). Apart from specialised fittings, Kunifer brake pipes, etc., the chassis will accept all the XJ running gear direct from a donor car without modification, the only specially supplied item being the 14gal Triumph 2000 fuel tank.

ABOVE. The Aristocat XK replica, utilising components from the XJ6.

Typical dashboard of an early Aristocat using Jaguar Mark II instrumentation.

Anthony Taylor's design of the Artistocat is based on the assumption that anyone with the slightest knowledge of car mechanics can build the kit simply by transferring parts from the donor car, but most customers tend to be Jaguar owners or enthusiasts.

The body, produced in fibreglass to resemble the XK 120 drophead coupé, is impregnated to give the desired colour and again will take most items from a donor XJ including lights, wheels, tyres, dashboard instruments, seats and door handles. All other items of trim including windscreen, bumpers and a choice of two different types of hood are supplied with the kit. Most owners tend to use a 4.2-litre XJ6 as a donor car and Series I or II models are the ideal, preferably with manual transmission. Anthony Taylor does buy in manual gearboxes to assist purchasers in converting automatic transmission cars as these are far more common. Building an Aristocat usually takes up to 300 man hours. On completion the owner has a sporting two-seater with more than a passing resemblance to the original XK but with the up-to-date performance and handling of a modern Jaguar — and all at a budget price. With a production run of two to three kits per month and over 200 cars now running, an Aristocat Owners Club has been formed and many drivers participate in competitive racing events. Insurance is reasonable at around group 5.

Aristocat is not the only builder to produce kits (or completed cars) based around XJ mechanicals. The replica scene has expanded rapidly over the recent years. Initially Mark II, S Type or 420 parts were used, but as these Jaguar models have increased in value and XJ saloons have depreciated, a thriving market for donor vehicles has been established.

Heritage Engineering produces SS100 and C Type replicas based on the XJ engine, gearbox and front and rear suspension. Although again produced with a fibreglass body these cars are not cheap to buy in kit form or completed but are of very high quality.

Another SS100 replica is the Steadman TS100 produced by Ottercraft in Cornwall. Although not as stunning a looker as the Heritage model, this replica will take XJ6 mechanicals direct from a donor car without any modification, so like the Aristocat this car is much wider than most kit cars. XJ mechanicals are also widely used in the building of AC Cobra replicas.

Production cars — some experiences

It is worth pausing a moment to review some of the standard production cars and their owners' opinions of them.

First the humble 2.8-litre XJ6 Series I: here I can speak from the experience of owning such a car, a manual/overdrive version of 1969 vintage finished in Racing Green with suede green interior. This was a very low-mileage example (only 23,000 miles on the clock when ten years old). Apart from the fact that the car had been extremely well looked after by its two previous owners this 2.8 was fortunate in still having its original engine, untouched and not yet fallen victim to the usual holed piston problem for which this model will always be remembered.

The car (like most 2.8s) had been sedately driven, and knowing something about the piston problem I decided to use it to the full, taking advantage of the manual gearbox and the willingness of the 2.8-litre unit to rev freely. The car was not particularly quick, but at cruising speeds of over 70mph on motorways it would amble along quite comfortably and in perfect quietness. Although sadly lacking the sometimes essential urge required for overtaking the engine was smooth and willing, but despite my efforts to avoid the dreaded piston problems, one day on a long trip averaging 60-70mph the

The author's 2.8-litre Series I, much underrated even if constant consideration has to be given to possible engine problems.

car suddenly started to misfire and puff out blue smoke from the exhausts. Further investigation revealed a hole in no. 3 piston, commiting another 2.8 to major engine repair. Whilst many 2.8s have been converted to 4.2s (or even 3.4s) there are some still in existence and running well. Perhaps today, with better lubricants and maintenance, the 2.8-litre engine is a more satisfactory unit.

Staying with the Series I cars but turning our attention to the opposite end of the spectrum I approached two owners of V12 cars, my elder brother Tony and "Jock" Hannah.

Tony Thorley owned a 1972 Series I V12 short-wheelbase model from new, using it for everyday transport until 1978, when the car was taken off the road and put into hibernation storage. Finished in powder blue with navy interior, this example came without air conditioning but retains all its original equipment even down to a complete tool roll. The biggest drawback of the early V12s is fuel consumption, or excess of it. This particular car used to give only around 11mpg even at a very leisurely pace. There is no doubting the smoothness of the V12 unit even in this carburated form, and the car drove so superbly well that it would be difficult to determine its age when compared with the very latest Sovereigns. Obviously the lack of sophisticated items like trip computer, cruise control and electric windows betray the age of what is otherwise a very modern car in excellent condition. The car is now in the author's hands – a change of owner but not a change of family.

ABOVE & RIGHT. Tony Thorley's XJ12 Series I, still in pristine condition, and virtually as new inside.

Jock Hannah's magnificent Series I Vanden Plas, a much loved car and increasing in value.

Jock Hannah is best known as the proprietor of A.W. Hannah Motors of Snaith on Humberside, specialists in the maintenance of XJs. He and his two sons make a winning team on the race track with an XJ Coupé. Jock's personal transport is a beautiful Series I Daimler Vanden Plas, again from 1973. He owned the car for a number of years and sold it to a local on the promise that if ever the car came up for sale, he should have first refusal to buy it back — which is exactly what he did a few years ago! Jock is one of those people who gets attached to things, and despite minor bodywork repairs the car is still very original and in superb condition, with all its original equipment. Now fitted with chromium plated ventilated wheels from a later XJ, this Vanden Plas looks excellent and is a real eyecatcher; Jock says there is something about the Vanden Plas with its uprated trim that makes it the equal of any other car, even a Rolls-Royce.

Now to the Series II models, not renowned for their longevity (except perhaps in Coupé form). Often poorly made, and with the passing years reduced to banger racing or dismantling as donor vehicles for replicas, these cars seem to be vanishing before our very eyes. I made contact with Frank Hastings from Leatherhead in Surrey, who owns a most magnificent example of the 4.2-litre manual/overdrive Series II saloon, happily registered 4200 XJ. This car was originally registered UWT 50N on 1st August 1974 with chassis no. 2T5162 DN, and was supplied new by Yorkshire dealers Ross Bros to the director of Brighouse Plastics Ltd. He used the car sparingly until he retired in 1980, when ownership was transferred to him personally. In 1987, when he sold the car to his niece's husband, it had only covered 5,149 miles from new! It was used daily after this until August 1988, when the car was sold again with a mileage of 14,800 and passed on via a Surrey dealer to a gentleman in London who changed it in late 1989 against a Daimler Double Six Vanden Plas. Frank Hastings bought the car from the same dealer in December 1989 with a total mileage of still only 16,035, exchanging a Series II Daimler Sovereign in the process.

After driving an automatic-transmission XJ for some nine years Frank finds the manual transmission generally preferable and is amazed by the responsiveness of the engine with the manual 'box. Apart from some heaviness of the clutch in traffic there is no doubt in Frank's mind that a manual-tranmission XJ is far superior to an automatic model. Whilst the transmission is not that smooth by some modern car standards, the engine is so flexible (it will easily pull away from 20mph in top) that gearchanges need not be frequent unless you want to take advantage of the acceleration available. Frank also finds fuel consumption vastly better, with 20mpg easily obtainable and more besides if he drives gently. Problems with the car have been few, mostly attributable to lack of use. Some hoses have needed changing and the odd item of chromium trim was tarnished. His extended experience of owning XJs has shown that these cars are reliable provided they are well maintained. Hoses, for example, must be changed every two to three years if you wish to avoid major problems which could cost up to £2,500. To Frank an XJ is the best value in the world!

We cannot pass by the Series II models without some reference to the Coupés, and here I spoke to Carl Hammond from Wetherby in West Yorkshire, who not only has an enthusiasm for the Coupé models but has actually started a small business restoring and selling them. His personal pride and joy is a Daimler Sovereign 4.2-litre Coupé finished in British racing green with tan interior. The car has undergone major restoration to bring it virtually to concours condition and at the time of our talk it was just going back on the road, resplendent with the optional chromium side strips and alloy wheels. Carl finds many Coupés in a very poor state of repair: they seem to rot in all the most unusual places, the doors drop, water collects in the body panels. These and wind noise are just a few of this model's problems. However, the rapidly increasing value of these fine cars has made them highly collectable and well worth spending a lot of money on. Carl maintains that given proper restoration with the right materials a Coupé is as

Frank Hastings' enthusiasm for Jaguars shows through in his car badges for three Jaguar orientated clubs!

Carl Hammond's Daimler Coupé now virtually restored.

fine a two-door Grand Touring car as anyone is likely to find, even taking into consideration other excellent models like the XJS or BMW 6 series.

Moving on to Series III models, firstly I approached Jack Stevens from London, a Jaguar enthusiast for many years and a stalwart of the Jaguar Enthusiasts' Club. Jack purchased his 3.4-litre XJ6 new from a local Jaguar dealer, smitten by the sage green colour. Having owned since new a 3.4-litre Mark II saloon, Jack took the plunge into the XJ scene just as the 3.4-litre model was being phased out and fell in love with his car at first sight in the showroom, adding only pepperpot alloy wheels to the overall specification, which he considers was quite comprehensive even for a 3.4. The 3.4 is quite slow even in this manual-transmission form when compared with the 4.2-litre XJ6 or even to his much earlier 3.4-litre Mark II but Jack, now retired, doesn't drive the car hard and when cruising on the motorway can hardly tell the difference in performance anyway. A genuine 16mpg is achieved and the 3.4 is very quiet and typically XJ in character, being smooth and extremely comfortable (particularly so with the woven seats).

Jack's 3.4 has completed 21,000 miles and has been relatively troublefree, except for a timing chain rattle, a replacement differential oil seal at 16,000 miles (said by the dealers to be normal), a water leak from the windscreen and, more surprisingly, the Michelin XWX tyres, which needed replacement at only 4,000 miles due to cracking of the walls. The car is serviced every 3,000 miles and has been completely wax injected to prevent rust. Jack also spends many hours cleaning the car to concours standard, recently taking Best XJ Award at a Jaguar Enthusiasts' Club concours.

After driving the car I can vouch for the typical XJ feel, and the performance is definitely up on the 2.8-litre engine. The interior is well finished (although in this case with woven cloth upholstery) but the veneering to the dashboard is straight grained walnut and not the usual burr associated with XJs.

Jack Stevens with his concours-winning XJ 3.4 Series III.

Another Jaguar Enthusiasts' Club member is John Reid, owner and everyday driver of a Daimler Double Six. John's interest in Jaguars began a few years ago when as an everyday car he purchased a 3.4-litre Series II XJ saloon. Unfortunately lack of power (it was an automatic) and poor quality trim put John off, so he went in search of a Jaguar providing the same degree of comfort and handling with more power, ending up with a 1978 Series II XJ12, again automatic and unusually for a V12 having cloth upholstery. John likes to use his cars and much liked the V12's silky performance but was always worried by the costs, particularly in fuel consumption, and so eventually traded the V12 in for a MG Maestro Turbo as everyday transport. This, while being quick off the mark and economical, was not a Jaguar and it wasn't long before John Reid was on the trail again. The performance of a secondhand XJ6 Series III which he tried was disappointing compared with the MG, so John decided to go back to the smoothness and flexibility of the V12, buying his current Daimler Double Six in 1986. It is a 1984 example with Vanden Plas upholstery and finished in Windsor Blue with doeskin interior.

Used as an everyday car the Daimler has provided excellent, virtually troublefree transport save for repeated problems with exhaust systems and the recent discovery of rust problems at the bottoms of the front wings and in the spare wheel well. Despite these upsets John finds the Double Six a superb grand tourer with excellent performance, an amazingly smooth automatic gearbox and magnificent handling and ride, even better than his other Jaguar, a 3.6 XJS cabriolet. John now intends to relegate the Double Six to a summer-only car and bring it back to pristine condition as soon as possible. It is a car the whole family can enjoy and there is no doubt that John intends keeping the Daimler for a long time to come.

To bring the story up to date I recently had the opportunity to drive and assess the very latest from the model range, the 1991 specification Jaguar

John Reid's everyday workhorse, his Daimler Double Six.

Sovereign. On first inspection one could easily pass by a 1991 XJ Series III saloon without comment (even on the £40,000 price tag) — the car has changed so little externally since the Series III's launch back in 1978. Perhaps today it doesn't confer the same prestige as a new Sovereign XJ40 or the latest BMW 750i, but one could argue the case for buying a secondhand Sovereign of, say, 1984 vintage and adding a personalised number plate. It would cost considerably less money and, due to the better quality of manufacture in the eighties, be a very usable and reliable motor car. It would look good too!

But there is nothing quite like the feel of a new car, and even at £45,000 the Daimler Double Six is exceptionally good value when compared with the latest S Class Mercedes or even the V12 BMW. The driver of a new Double Six (usually a company director or chief executive) wants not only quality and luxury but power and controllability. All these are offered by the Daimler. Now an elderly design, the Series III has been brought into the nineties with ABS braking, lead-free fuel and computerised air conditioning. The ride is as good as ever, lead-free petrol seems to have no adverse effect on performance, and the revised ratios of the GM400 gearbox have improved responsiveness. It is not hard to see why the V12 is still popular, yet with the imminent arrival of XJ41 (the V12-engined XJ40) even the Double Six is finally doomed to extinction. Will there ever be another car quite like it? If you have never drive a V12 Series III saloon, you still have a treat and surprise in store.

The very latest V12 Jaguar, by courtesy of Hatfields Jaguar dealership in Sheffield.

ABOVE. One of the
remaining XJC
Broadspeed racers, now in
private hands.

BELOW. Andrew Jeffery
putting his Series II saloon
through its paces at
Oulton Park in Cheshire.

Experienced XJ racer
Andrew Hannah with his
highly modified XJ
Coupé.

PC Thompson with the
South Yorkshire
Constabulary XJ6s.

The Avon XJ Series III
estate car conversion –
hearse-like from the rear.

ABOVE. Cabriolet
International conversion
of a Daimler Sovereign
Series III.

BELOW. The XJ concours
scene still has room for
prospective participants.

XJ racing

The Broadspeed V12 Coupés

The name of Jaguar has long been associated with racing, an important part of the company's history. The Jaguar reputation had rested for years on the Le Mans successes of the fifties and on the many exploits of Mark IIs in the early sixties, but apart from abortive attempts at a comeback with the XJ13 V12 prototype the company had let the racing side slip into oblivion.

With the advent of the production V12 engines in the E Type and XJ saloons a perfect opportunity presented itself to enter the racing scene with an immensely strong engine that could easily be modified to produce more power. Jaguar were still not happy at the prospect even though Ralph Broad from the Broadspeed organisation in Southam (already campaigning the Triumph Dolomite team for British Leyland) had hinted at his enthusiasm. He believed it would be possible to raise the output of the V12 engine to over 500bhp and on the introduction of the XJS had offered to take up the challenge, but was rebuffed by the Jaguar management.

The change to Leyland management brought a new resolve to sell more cars and in March 1976 Leyland announced Jaguar's return to racing, in the European Touring Car Race Championship, using a V12-engine car — not the newly released XJS as had been expected but the XJ12 Coupé. Broadspeed were commissioned to carry out the development work necessary to produce a suitable racing car from standard XJ Coupé bodyshells supplied by Jaguar.

It must be said that Broadspeed had to significantly modify the Coupés, which affected their reliability. For example, the V12 engine was bored out to increase capacity from 5,343 to 5,416cc, giving dimensions of 90.6 × 70.0mm, with a 12:1 compression ratio, and was equipped with Lucas mechanical fuel injection taking air from a specially constructed ram-effect plenum chamber. Although the crankshaft had to remain the same the connecting rods were lightened, peened, X-rayed and fitted with heavy duty big end bolts. Many other parts were bought in from Cosworth to accompany other modifications by Broadspeed including specially forged pistons with the combustion chambers carried part in the head and part in the piston. Deeply recessed valves operated in bronze guides and seats, and camshafts were machined from solid billets.

XJ Broadspeed Coupe:
press launch picture, 23
March 1976.

An estimated 550bhp was produced by the Broadspeed-modified V12 at 8,000rpm, with peak torque at 5,750rpm. A single-plate hydraulic clutch with 780lb pressure diaphragm spring was made up by Automotive Products and mated to a standard XJS Jaguar close ratio gearbox. There was a choice of three sets of gear ratios and seven final drive ratios from 3.54:1 to 5.38:1. Both gearbox and differential had their own oil cooling systems.

Massive four-pot Lockheed calipers were fitted to the initially water-cooled ventilated disc brakes on the Coupés and had a mammoth task stopping these cars under racing conditions. The water cooling system was activated by a foot switch in the cockpit which directed jets of cold water into the eye of the discs. To aid cooling large ducting hoses directed air from the rear of the vehicle via the boot to the inboard rear brakes.

Suspension was basically standard XJ but at the front double coil springs were used with specially made up Armstrong dampers. At the rear ultra-wide wishbones combined with special driveshafts to locate the wheels. Twin adjustable coil springs and dampers were also used with tubular driveshafts.

The Coupés were extensively modified inside, with racing seats, roll over bars, etc., but retained standard production door trims and dashboard main area. Externally, the standard steel shell was lightened, and reinforced with a massive rollcage and side barrier system welded up for rigidity. Front and rear bulkheads were sealed against fire and all electrical wiring was cotton-covered. Other alterations included extra radiator intakes at the front, air dam, and extended wheel-arches to accommodate the oversize Dunlop racing tyres and specially constructed alloy wheels. The original colour scheme was predominantly white with red and blue flashing. Whilst the Jaguar leaping cat was well sited on the the rear wings the Leyland Cars name and logo predominated, for the cars were seen as a method of promoting the whole group rather than just Jaguar.

Massive specially constructed fuel tank, which could be filled without lifting the boot lid.

Interior of the Broadspeed Coupe, retaining elements of the standard dash layout.

After announcement in March 1976 Leyland intended to enter their first race with an XJ12 Coupé at Easter, and although Broad was already well on with the development of the new car they had experienced major problems, blowing up three engines and crashing one car during testing when a wheel broke up. Despite other announcements that the XJ Coupés would make their début at meets in May and July, the car's first race participation did not come until September at the Tourist Trophy round at Silverstone. Not only was Silverstone Broadspeed's local circuit, it was on British soil and the T.T. race after the war had seen the debut of the XK120s, so it was an excellent launch pad for the Jaguar (or should we say British Leyland) offensive.

Jaguar enthusiasts were captivated by the possibility of Jaguar returning to racing, so much so that droves of them turned out for the Tourist Trophy meeting that September. With such devotion to the marque and with drivers like Derek Bell and David Hobbs in charge of the Big Cat, things were looking good for Jaguar. The Coupé took a front row position on the grid after qualifying at 1 minute 36.72 seconds, faster than the opposing BMWs. The Jaguar led the race for the first nine laps but handling started to deteriorate quickly due to problems with a mixed batch of tyres. Eventually one tyre gave out and five laps were lost. Although the car returned to the race, twenty laps later a wheel was lost due to a collapsed driveshaft. Despite these problems the Jaguar did manage to create a new official Group Two record lap of 1 minute 38.50 seconds, and British Leyland boss Alex Park was highly delighted with the first outing.

This was the British Leyland Coupé's only race in 1976 as Broad wanted time for further development, and the BL management agreed. John Davenport was appointed BL's competition director and the driver line-up for the 1977 season was decided: Derek Bell, Andy Rouse, John Fitzpatrick and Tim Schenken. External modifications to the car included a completely new paint scheme in revised Leyland Motorsport colours, predominantly blue and white, with a new boot-mounted spoiler and specially manufactured 19in wheels. Many other (undocumented) changes were made, including the removal of power assistance from the steering.

The first race of the 1977 European Car Championship was in March at Monza, and the two Coupés appeared against stiff competition from BMW in several forms including a brand new 3.2-litre from the Bavarian Alpina racing company. Oil starvation problems affected both marques during practice and Jaguar only had one spare engine, which was fitted before the start to the first car with problems.

For over twenty laps the Fitzpatrick car led the race, closely followed by the Alpina BMW until it retired with head gasket failure. After only an hour

XJ Coupé in later racing trim complete with boot spoiler at Monza in 1977.

Nurburgring, and yet
another engine change.

The Coupe on fine form at
Zandvoort in 1977.

of racing, however, the Jaguar had to retire with major oil pressure loss under severe braking caused by the wet-sump lubrication system. The car had performed well up to that time and must be considered a credit to Broadspeed.

The second round of the Championship took place in Salzburg, where the two Jaguars gained first and fourth positions on the grid. The first car retired after only eleven laps with driveshaft failure, and the other, which had been leading the race for twenty laps, pulled into the pits after a stone pierced the radiator, when it was also discovered that a driveshaft was about to shear.

The driveshaft problem persisted despite testing in Coventry, and the Big Cats did not enter the next two rounds of the Championship, but they did turn out for the Czechoslavakian round at Brno, where the British cars could hope for a good race on the long, fast and relatively straight circuit ideally suited to them.

During practice the cars reached speeds of up to 170mph and they shared the front row of the grid. They led in the early stages but the first car (driven by Derek Bell) had eventually to retire due to gearbox seizure. The other car (driven by Fitzpatrick) suffered a high speed blow-out which ripped away substantial chunks of the rear bodywork and caused damage to the suspension. After repairs the car returned to the fray but was suffering clutch overheating. If finished the race in sixteenth position overall and third in its class.

At the next challenge at the Nurburgring the Jaguar practice sessions proved a disaster, with no less than two engine replacements, a head replacement and fuel metering problems. Despite such happenings one Jaguar ended up on the front row of the grid, the other on the third row, and new tactics of driving steadily to finish the race were adopted. Despite this Fitzpatrick produced a very creditable first lap, averaging 100mph, with the second-place BMW a good twelve seconds behind him, but sadly on the second lap his engine gave up, retiring him from the race. The second Jaguar, driven by Bell and Rouse, behaved reasonably well, taking second place to a BMW, although to be absolutely honest this was a poor result as the BMW team had been experiencing major problems themselves, limiting their speed and performance.

For August at Zandvoort one of the Jaguars had been converted to dry-sump lubrication in view of changes in the race regulations. Problems with the system occurred numerous times, eventually losing it the race, while the other Jaguar's final drive disintegrated, sinking BL's hopes completely. The following Dutch race also proved a disaster for Jaguar.

For the next round Jaguar returned home to Silverstone for the Tourist Trophy race in September. Jaguar produced the two fastest practice laps at an average of over 110mph, probably helped by new stiffer-wall tyres. The best placed Jaguar, the dry-sump car, crashed early on after a hub sheared. The second (wet-sump) car carried on well, maintaining a 27-second lead over the nearest BMW, but was severely handicapped, as the Jaguars had always been, by the sheer number of pitstops required to take on fuel. With the onset of a downpour the track became very greasy, and the Jaguar eventually span off and crashed.

In the final round of the series the Jaguars suffered yet again from tyre and engine problems, and BL decided to retire from the racing scene. In hindsight the cars were still underdeveloped, overweight and not sufficiently fuel efficient. Broadspeed maintained that given more racing experience and development the XJ12 Coupés could have gone on to better things, but Leyland had had enough despite the enthusiasm of everyone concerned, not least the Jaguar fans who had virtually "willed" the cars to succeed. It is a tribute to Tom Walkinshaw and his TWR Race Organisation that they later developed the XJS so successfully for the same race championship series.

Club racing

XJ saloons have had very little involvement in serious racing since that time although the XJS (based on the V12 engine and XJ swb floorpan) has seen much active service on the circuits of the world. It has been left to enthusiastic owners to race XJs on our circuits, initially in the XJ Challenge series run by the Jaguar Drivers Club racing register. Since these beginnings in the early eighties many Series Is and IIs have been seen competing in race events. Yet it is surprising that there are not more individuals entering Jaguar racing with XJs, for the cars' excellent handling in standard form makes them virtually ideal.

I took time out to visit and talk to one of the XJ racing brigade, Andrew Jefferies (General Manager of Hatfields, Jaguar main dealers in South Yorkshire), who campaigns his Series II XJ6 saloon in club events. Andrew started racing with a 420 saloon but after a major accident requiring a total rebuild of the car decided to turn his attentions to the XJ series. He felt that being in plentiful supply at very cheap prices and with an endless availability of parts (as well as interchangeability) and ease of repair (the body panels being bolted on), the XJ saloon was an ideal basis for racing on a tight budget.

One of the few Series I XJs ever involved in racing, here seen at a 1983 Oulton Park club meeting.

Series II cars are the cheapest to buy and needing a manual-transmission version Andrew placed an advertisement in various magazines for a 4.2-litre. That was easy enough but he had no response! Despite contacts in the motor trade nothing was forthcoming until he saw a Series II manual model in his home town of Sheffield, belonging to a local chemist. After negotiating a deal Andrew bought the car, which needed some remedial work, and then set about converting it to racing specification.

Preparation of an XJ for racing can be made very simple and straightforward. Starting with the suspension, the front springs of the XJ6 can be replaced by V12 items (stiffer and stronger) slightly cut down to lower the car. Some think that Daimler DS420 limousine springs can be used on the XJ as they are stronger but these units will *not* interchange with XJ springs. The rear suspension is also lowered slightly to balance the front and all shock absorbers are replaced by competition type Koni adjustable units.

It is perfectly possible to retain the standard 4.2-litre XJ power unit for racing purposes, but Andrew substituted his old 420 engine, which had been carefully rebuilt and balanced. Some gas-flowing of the head had been carried out and the original twin SU carburettors had been replaced by triple SUs and adapted manifolds from a 4.2-litre Mark X, all of which fits into the engine bay easily without any unsightly bonnet modifications or movement of ancillary equipment.

As the braking system in the XJ saloon is already excellent little updating should be required. Andrew had his brakes rebuilt but included competition specification pads. The one Achilles heel of XJ brakes is the lack of adequate cooling in racing conditions for the inboard rear discs. To overcome this Andrew adopted the same policy as Tom Walkinshaw's XJS team, removing panels from the boot floor and always running with the boot lid slightly open. This creates sufficient air circulation to keep the brakes cool. Some racing people fit air scoops to aid cooling but if these are not correctly designed they can pick up hot air from the exhaust system and have quite the wrong effect! At the front, holes have been cut in the body to aid cooling of the front discs.

Alloy wheels are fitted along with completely standard XJS (current size) tyres. These, being of slightly lower profile, help to compensate for the high axle ratio on many XJs. The regulation power/fuel cut-off switch, taped headlights, lap and diagonal seat belts, etc., are included in the modifications (in this class of racing roll-over bars are not required). Andrew has now gone one better and had a four-point driver's seat belt fitted. There are also minor matters that must be attended to before the Jaguar goes racing: all doors must be unlocked, the ignition switch must be clearly marked for "off" position, and all windows must be closed.

In its present lightly modified form Andrew's XJ6 can hold its own against the competition: other XJs and of course XJSs, mostly with automatic transmission. Although the V12s are quicker than the XJ6s, in the hands of a competent driver the XJ6 can stay with them. As for cost, purchase, remedial bodywork and preparation for racing set Andrew back around £3,500, not a princely sum in racing terms and now representing what must be the best value for money for anyone wishing to participate in racing on a

tight budget. Apart from fuel and race expenses (perhaps £100 for two races at a meeting) there is little else to worry the would-be entrant, though XJ tyres can be expensive. Andrew suggests always carrying a spare set, one well worn for good dry conditions, another with a good depth of tread for wet days. Tyres can be consumed by a large and heavy car like the XJ in a matter of hours!

A nice sequence of shots showing how hard an XJ driver can work, taken at Silverstone.

A well prepared Series II with rear doors welded up for extra structural rigidity.

One of the few Series III saloons to compete in racing.

The reason why Andrew decided on an XJ6 rather than a vastly more competitive V12 car was really one of cost. The XK six-cylinder engine is immensely strong but is easily repairable, and with so many around after 40 years of production even a wrecked engine can be relatively inexpensively replaced. Replacement of a V12, on the other hand, is a horrendously costly affair — all the more appalling if it arises from something trifling like a leaking water hose leading to seizure.

As for sponsorship, this type of racing requires that the vehicle be a road-going car, so full sponsorship is not possible, although minor assistance may be available by way of free oil, etc.

If you want to go a step further it is possible to prepare an XJ for a more competitive form of racing, as have the Hannah family from Humberside. Their V12 Coupé has been substantially modified, with high lift cams, modified fuel injection, lightened body panels, specially adapted suspension and so on, to the point where their car is not only competitive against many muscle cars (including modified XJSs) but has regularly come away from meetings with fastest lap times. All of which goes to show that the XJ saloon can be competitive as a racing car despite BL's abortive involvement in the past. It is a pity that more people do not take to the tracks with an XJ, but with the advent of new racing series and opportunities I am sure we will see more XJs competing in the near future.

Jock and Adrian Hannah
with their highly
competitive XJC V12.

LEFT. Interior of the
Hannah V12 Coupé with
rollover cage and racing
seat.

BELOW. The Hannah V12
Coupé taking another lap
record at Donington in
1990.

Purchase, restoration and modification

In this chapter we will look at the purchase of an XJ, the points to watch when considering restoration or renovation and modifications that can be made to improve the cars.

Purchase

When it comes to purchasing an XJ saloon one can be forgiven for thinking that it must be a relatively easy task, for after all the XJ appears to have everything going for it. Firstly it has been produced in large numbers (more than any other Jaguar saloon) from 1968 to the present day. Secondly there is a vast array of models and engine configurations to choose from. Thirdly, because the cars are still in production today parts and spares are easily obtainable. And lastly, cars produced in the Egan era are generally considered to be of the highest quality and will probably give little trouble in any respect.

These are sweeping statements and largely true, but many other factors need to be considered very carefully. Buying an XJ is no different from buying any secondhand or even classic car. There are and will be for some time to come a lot of cars for sale, many of which will have been poorly maintained. The earliest cars are now well over 20 years old and will have passed through several hands before you get them. Even the latest cars may have passed through dealers, auctions and more dealers before you see them for sale. Despite stiffer regulations late cars may have been "clocked" to reduce the mileage shown and service histories may have been falsified. Yet, leaving aside such gloom and despondency, provided an XJ is well looked after and properly maintained it is a great car and one that will give hundreds of thousands of miles of pleasure. No other car can offer such excellent value for money in comfort, handling, quietness and performance.

Let us start with the choice of model: with three Series to choose from, four engine configurations, two wheelbases, two or four doors and even two marques, where does one start?

Your first choice could be to select the marque to suit your taste. Realistically there should be little to choose between a Daimler or Jaguar except that Vanden Plas models (with the superior interior trim) are only available in Daimler form. In the case of Coupés the V12 Daimlers are the rarest and perhaps therefore will offer slightly better investment potential in the future. But if you do not have a marque preference then ignore the radiators and just buy the *best* for the money you have to spend.

Next, do you really want a Coupé or are you content with a four-door saloon? Coupés are already increasing in price whereas saloons are either static, rising slightly (earlier cars) or still depreciating! Coupés are rarer in the main and to most tastes look the nicest. You lose little in interior space although some parts (particularly door panels and rear wings) are very hard to come by.

Staying with the Coupé, the Daimler 4.2 is the most common and the Daimler V12 the rarest, but again if you intend to buy the best car you can get on your budget don't bother which model you end up with. Coupés can be prone to more than their fair share of problems and as Jaguar never got them 100% right you need not expect your purchase to be A1 either. But a good Coupé can look magnificent, especially on a warm day with all the windows wound down out of sight.

If your taste is for the saloons, then the choice is enormous. Perhaps it is best to decide on the Series in the first instance. Series I cars are now getting more difficult to find, particularly the short-wheelbase versions and even more so V12 versions on that wheelbase. As the last Series IIs were produced in the mid-seventies it is not so easy to find one-owner, low-mileage examples, although the odd one does turn up. The vast majority of cars on offer in this Series are 4.2s, the smaller-engined 2.8s having long past gone to the scrapyards or been fitted with other engines as a result of the all-too-common piston failures.

Interestingly, 2.8s usually survived in better overall condition (bar the engines!) than 4.2s because they were bought by the more sedate type of owner when new. It was not unusual up to a few years ago to find excellent low-mileage 2.8s around but these days, whilst some are still for sale, they are not in as new condition any more and are usually treated with some suspicion, the price being affected accordingly. However, if you don't mind taking a chance with a 2.8, they can prove exceptional value for money as a first entry into the XJ scene.

Series I 4.2s are common enough but again genuine low-mileage examples are very few and far between. Basically the 4.2 engine of that era is a very good unit and will last a long time, but values are now starting to rise so do not expect bargain basement prices.

V12 cars in Series I form are getting rare and a short-wheelbase example in good condition is well worth considering if you can find one. The frontal treatment of the V12 is more attractive but the early V12's fuel consumption is not. Everyday use of one of these cars at what can easily be single-figure mpg is appallingly expensive. The level of trim of the early cars can also put some off. These V12s do offer excellent potential for investment, however, and look well with a good paint job and chromium-plated wheels.

Series II cars need a totally different approach. They have always been the least loved of the range, many having been badly manufactured and sent out from the Factory with poor quality control and/or ill-conceived, garish colour schemes (inside and out!). Mechanically the Series IIs were not that

Series II models can prove excellent value for money but are notorious for poor quality workmanship. Note the fit of the boot lid on this excellent original car.

hot either, with a noticeable deterioration in the quality of the engines, and poorly chosen axle ratios which deprived many cars of Jaguar type performance in top-speed terms.

Series II saw the introduction of the 3.4-litre model, mostly supplied in base form without leather, electric windows and the like. These are still not worth a lot and are dropping in price but like the 2.8 can prove good value.

The 4.2s are again the easiest to find, with various trim levels, and although rapidly declining in numbers can still be bought for very little money. One of these could be ideal as everyday transport, as a donor car for a replica or as a basis for restoration. It is still possible (just!) to find a really excellent example like Frank Hastings' one (mentioned in the last but one chapter) or like the one I recently saw at a Jaguar dealership, owned by one man from new and only just changed for a new XJ40! Such cars will fetch much higher prices than some seven-year-old Series IIIs.

As for the V12 versions, Series II saw the introduction of fuel injection, which helped in a small way to improve fuel economy. Series II versions of the Vanden Plas can also be a good buy as they are usually the cheapest VDP cars available, with good potential for investment and enjoyment. Because of the more careful finishing of the VDPs, they have also stood up to the years better.

In conclusion, therefore, as Series II cars are not popular at the moment they must offer good value: buy if the condition is right.

Series III cars are a totally different case. The enthusiast would see the Series I model as the "purest" of the XJs but the Series III range offers a vast choice to the prospective purchaser. Having been in production since 1978 more cars from this range have been produced than from any other. With many trim levels and a very wide band of prices, these cars will suit anyone's tastes.

The 3.4s, again the least loved, do in the main offer a better level of trim than the Series II 3.4s. They remain relatively underpowered and apart from the very last models still don't have the highest level of equipment even if factory extra-cost options were specified by the original owner. They are, however, very cheap to buy at the moment.

Series III 4.2s are the most common and a late-seventies or early-eighties car can be bought at a very attractive price indeed. The best of the range would either be a late model Sovereign with the fully-loaded specification or a Vanden Plas. Good late-model Sovereigns are rapidly levelling out in price which must make them a good bet for the future. The 4.2 litre engines of this era, however, are not renowned for their longevity. Most seem to need a mechanical rebuild before 100,000 miles no matter how good the service history or owner/driver care. The Series III V12 is of course still available today. Early cars without the "Fireball" head are lacking in fuel economy but are marginally faster than the later cars. The post-HE models are generally a better buy and in Sovereign, Double Six or Vanden Plas form are the best value. Even a one or two year old example will fetch substantially less than half its new cost today. Although V12s are still readily available on the secondhand market, the Sovereigns and Double Sixes like the 4.2-litre equivalents are flattening out on price and seem to sell very easily. The prestige of the V12 engine does wonders for the small businessman's ego, especially when such a car is cheaper to buy secondhand than a new middle of the range Ford and with private plates cannot easily be dated! All Series IIIs after 1984 were undoubtedly better built in the Egan era's "Pursuit of Excellence". Very early Series IIIs were notorious for bad paintwork and poor electrics just as the Series IIs were known for bad reliability and rust!

Assessment and restoration

The restoration or refurbishment of an XJ saloon must not be considered lightly. The cars are relatively well built and many parts are available but they are sophisticated vehicles by any standards. Even if you have experience of restoring other Jaguars like the E Type or Mark II the complications and costs of an XJ may confound you.

Jaguars have always had a bad reputation for rust and while XJs were better built than many cars one has to bear in mind that like all Jaguars they were built down to a price. So XJs are prone to rust and it is very rare to find one without some body rot somewhere. Having said that, later models are much better protected and will last up to five or six years without showing signs of significant rust problems.

In short, later Series IIs are worse than the earlier cars as far as bodywork is concerned. Series IIs are generally the worst of all in general bodywork, quality control and paint finish. Early Series III cars are just as prone as Series IIs to body rot and have their own problems with paintwork, as Jaguar during this period were experiencing major problems with paint crazing. For quality of paint finish and rust protection the last of the line should be far superior to all other models. Perhaps the Vanden Plas models should also be given consideration for their superior finish, Series I versions being literally "hand finished".

The pointers to look for when inspecting bodywork include the leading edges of the front wings above the headlights. Water and mud are constantly thrown up into this area and collect, forming a blockage eventually leading

A tyical example of an elderly Series I saloon, which could still be driveable, but those rust patches on the bodywork may well and probably do indicate major problems underneath.

Another Series I, this time a Daimler, which looks better than the Jaguar but note the usual rust in the headlamp area. Such rust usually means there is much more unseen. Note the low ride height of this car, showing signs of worn out springs, a common fault on older XJs.

This is how it all starts!

to bubbles appearing in the paintwork. The wheelarch lips also collect mud leading to bubbling of the paint. Rust also affects the rear bottom half of the front wings, behind which water collects. Front wings are easily changed as they are bolted on, but in the case of Series I models "new" wings are very hard to come by.

The under-bumper front valance is a major cause of rust, especially in the seams where it joins the front wings and also because this area gets neglected (out of sight, out of mind). The main cross member lies just under the front valance and should be inspected to establish whether the car has previously had a "shunt", been badly repaired or rusted.

Very early Series Is had a simple chromium-plated headlamp surround, taken directly from the 420 saloon. These pit quite badly but are easy to replace. All later models have air intake grilles in the chrome surrounds of the outer headlamps and these are easy to acquire as replacements. Other plated parts for the front are relatively easy to obtain. The Series I XJ6 grille can be difficult to find and is again often neglected as it requires regular detail cleaning to keep in first class condition. The bumper plating on Series II models was particularly poor and never seemed to last long.

On all XJs the "A" post (front windscreen/door pillar) is prone to rotting out to such an extent that the scuttle can also be rusting below the paintwork unseen. This area is obviously vulnerable to water running down the gutters

ABOVE. Water and mud will collect in the bottom rear of the front wing, eventually rusting out the panelling. This wing did not look bad apart from severe blistering on the exterior paintwork, and even the inner wing panel looks reasonable upon first glance. With part of the wing cut away the rest of the problem becomes apparent . . .

ABOVE RIGHT . . . and this what lurks behind.

RIGHT. Underneath the surface rust on the front of the sill lurk major panel problems, often covered up quickly to make good at little cost.

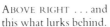

ABOVE. The good thing about XJs is that most parts are still readily available from autojumbles, scrap yards or even from the dealers themselves.

RIGHT. At the front, with the bumper removed, the cross member can be seen, in this case severely corroded and dangerous.

A very dangerous symptom is rust around the bottom of the windscreen pillar and in the scuttle area. This windscreen could fall out, and in the event of the car rolling over the screen pillars would collapse.

and weakness here can be dangerous in the event of the car rolling over as the 'screen pillars can collapse. The rusting can continue right down the "A" post inside the front wing area, again unnoticed until a wing needs replacement.

At the side of the car the sills obviously are prone to rust, particularly where they meet the front and rear wings. Look particularly at the bottom of the rear door aperture. The inner sills will also be a constant cause of concern and need correct treatment to ensure an effective and safe repair. The bottoms of the doors rust through just as on any other older car. Coupé doors are now very difficult to get hold of as are rear doors for short-wheelbase saloons. The Coupé also suffers badly from door drop through the sheer weight of the extra-wide doors. Rear wings do not escape rust either, particularly around the wheel arch edges and where the wing meets the sill. Again, Coupé rear wings are the most difficult to get hold of. On earlier saloons rust can show in bubbles midway between the fuel filler cap and rear edge on top and between the rear wing and rear valance. These valances below the rear wings and rear bumper are major areas of regular rust. The rear valance again gets neglected because of its out-of-the-way position and collects a good deal of mud thrown up from the rear wheels. It is also easily damaged when replacing exhausts. Both the valance and the

Water has collected in the bottom of the rear wing of this Coupé behind the door shut face, causing devastation.

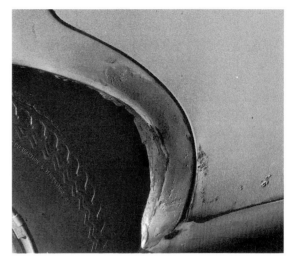

ABOVE LEFT. Rusting from the inside at the bottoms of the doors is a common occurrence on most older cars.

ABOVE. Rust around the rear wheel-arch is common on XJs. This arch has been filled at some time and rust is coming through again.

LEFT. Just how bad things can get: this wheel-arch has disintegrated, and there is rot everywhere.

A very common area of concern is in the "D" post area where the sill meets the rear wheel-arch. A very small amount of rust here usually hides more problems once you start to clear away the paint.

ABOVE. An extreme case of rear wing malady, inside and out.

ABOVE LEFT. Rear inner wing and sill problems are common too.

Most XJs have some rust on the rear wing edges where they meet the bumper bar.

panels below the rear wings are only bolted on so are easily changed. Front and rear wing wheel arch lips rot but wheel arch panels are readily available for welding into place.

The roof can suffer at the rear as a result of water seeping down the channels but cars fitted with vinyl roofs, e.g. Coupés and Vanden Plas cars, have a particular problem. Water seeps under the vinyl and starts rust without being noticed. The first signs of trouble are usually bubbles in the vinyl covering, the most common places being around sun-roof apertures, at the front near the windscreen and in the rear quarters.

The boot lid can easily rust at its bottom edge as water collects in the rubbers. Chromium plating at the rear is also particularly poor on some Series Is and most Series IIs. On Series I cars with the number plate light in the bumper, this light unit is very prone to collecting water and rusting out.

LEFT. A rare sight, XJ Coupé rear wings, now in very short supply.

ABOVE. A magnificent XJ bodyshell, virtually as new; such items can still be found for that XJ restoration, perhaps a better prospect than replacing all the rotted areas.

LEFT. Vinyl roofs are a common cause of rust as damp can get trapped beneath them.

The double-skinned edge of the boot lid holds damp and rusts out.

Other parts of the exterior trim keep reasonably well. Series II front side lights, being in poor quality plastic, do give constant trouble and the drain holes beside the petrol tank fillers often get clogged up, causing water to collect and eventually enter the tanks. Some windscreen and rear window brightwork is difficult to come by, and beware the very poor quality exterior front door locks used on many Series Is and IIs— they wear very quickly. The plastic badges fitted to most XJs were very cheap items and often break away, particularly those on the boot showing model and litre designation. On very late XJs these were replaced by much better solid metal badges.

On all saloons the doors should shut well and seldom require major adjustment. The boot again should shut easily, only being affected when someone unknowingly (despite warning labels in the boot) slams it shut. The bonnet is a very flexible affair and often gets out of alignment, leading to one of the catches flying open when it shouldn't or chipping of the paintwork on the bonnet and wings. The correct way to close an XJ bonnet is to handle it from the front centre and not from the side rear.

No XJ has ever been fitted from new with a leaping cat mascot although many have been added. The addition of such an item is strictly speaking illegal as the Construction and Use Regulations specifically dictate that unless fitted as standard from new, it is illegal to fit such items as an afterthought. Many Daimlers featured a central bonnet strip not interchangeable with any other Jaguar model.

Inside the boot there is more rust to be found. Removing the spare wheel reveals how badly the well is rusted — even on cars only three years old!

The interior of the XJ usually wears well. Leather trim is obviously expensive to replace and the ventilated upholstery of Series I models can cause particular problems as it is not so easily replaceable. The padded, flocked backs of the front seats often discolour or lose their shape, especially if

LEFT. This is the interior of the spare wheel area in the boot, showing the uncovered fuel pumps. Note the large rotted out area in the floor common on XJs, even late model Series IIIs.

BELOW. Beautifully restored, this is what the same area should look like.

they have been removed several times for any reason. Cloth seats have their own problems, particularly on Series II models, as they collect dirt and static and do not clean up very well. Carpets can be in a poor state on some models not just through constant use but because they were not always of the highest quality, but they are easily replaceable. The cost of replacing interior trim items need not be too great as there are plenty of cars being broken up for parts. Even if the colour is not what you need, treatments like Vinylcote can change it to suit your requirements.

Woodwork was best on the Series I models, that on most Series IIs and Series IIIs being veneered on to thinner wood panels. Vanden Plas cars are generally finished to a higher standard and all XJ woodwork wears better than that of many earlier Jaguar saloons. The same cannot be said of some of the other equipment, instruments and switches for example having been produced in poor quality plastics and in the case of some Series IIs with cheap bright trimming. Series I cars also suffered from the ventilator outlets on the dashboard top roll warping, particularly if the heater was constantly on "hot".

Electrical equipment fitted to XJs has always been suspect, even on the latest models. In all the XJs I have ever driven I can count on the fingers of one hand the times both horns worked! The electrics are very sophisticated and will give constant trouble, particularly fuses, cruise control, air conditioning,

A well prepared engine bay, though this owner has chosen to chromium plate and polish many parts of the engine which normally would not be.

electric aerial, electric windows and even lights. The most reliable items appear to be the trip computer, clock and ignition.

Mechanically an XJ can be a very expensive proposition. Starting with the engine, the earlier 4.2-litre units are very reliable and if well maintained should be good for at least 100,000 miles before major overhaul. Later units are not known for their high mileage capabilities and many Series III engines do not even manage 80,000 before giving trouble, but if well maintained and treated with proper respect can fare a lot better. The most common faults on XK engines are cracking of the top face of the block, timing chain rattles and poor oil pressure.

The oil pressure gauge should read around 40psi at 3,000rpm when the engine is hot, although pressure may go up to the top of the gauge when the engine is cold and may drop down to about 15psi on tickover. Timing chain wear is indicated by a metallic rattle from the front of the engine. There are two chains: the top one is easily adjustable with the appropriate tool but adjusting the bottom one calls for a good deal of dismantling.

A good XK engine should never be noisy although one may expect, and even welcome, some slight tappet noise. A propensity to use and lose oil is quite normal, so don't expect more than 2-300mpp and always expect some leakage on to the garage floor. However, a major leak from the rear of the engine can mean that the rear main bearing oil seal has expired. This is a big job to put right. The engines do stay very clean so leaks from the water system or the power steering can easily be spotted. If any water is getting into the oil a leaking head gasket can be diagnosed. Lastly, on early cars the radiator is particularly small and can allow the engine to overheat, causing the cylinder head to warp.

Cooling systems on all engines must contain a rust inhibitor, usually in the form of anti-freeze. As the cylinder head is aluminium, interaction can take place causing severe corrosion of the waterways, a major and regular problem on XK engines.

The 2.8-litre engines of the Series I range have been covered in some detail in an earlier chapter: regardless of upkeep they are prone to piston failure. The 3.4 is a relatively strong engine and should give little trouble if well maintained.

All XK six-cylinder engines should run smoothly on tickover. If vibration or unevenness is evident the carburettors may be out of balance or carburettor parts worn. Under hard acceleration or deceleration some blue-grey haze may be observed from the exhausts, which is normal, but if the exhausts smoke all the time the engine is well worn.

The V12 engine is obviously a lot more complex and poor maintenance can have horrendous financial consequences. Having said that, the engine is very strong and certainly understressed. Corrosion inhibitors are vital as the whole engine is aluminium based. Overheating can cause heads to warp and literally weld themselves to the block. Water pump problems used to be common on V12 engines and any sign of trouble in this area or leaks from the proliferation of pipes and hoses under the bonnet must be seen to immediately. An overheated V12 engine can cost a fortune to rebuild.

The V12 does not use as much oil as the XK engine but beware of extremely high oil consumption or severe oil leaks, particularly from the rear of the engine. There may be a lot of minor oil leaks from oil pipes and unions but these will usually require little attention to put right. Oil pressure should be 60-80psi at between 3,500 and 4,000rpm.

Common electrical problems on V12 cars involve the fuel injection system and the electronic ignition. Ignition amplifiers often cause trouble but are easily replaced. As on XJ6s, other electrical faults are frequent.

After passing through various owners' hands a V12 engine can easily get neglected. All the ancillary equipment and plumbing on top of it make virtually all items difficult to work on, particularly the exhaust manifolds. On earlier Series I XJ12s without air conditioning or fuel injection accessibility is rather better.

The V12 engine should always run smoothly even when starting from ice cold. For the uninitiated fault detection is problematical as the engine is so powerful and smooth that it is difficult to establish what, if anything, could be wrong!

As for ancillary equipment on both XJ6s and V12s, problems are often experienced with the power steering and air conditioning. The power steering operates on a rack and can be expensive to replace if play is evident. The pump itself if excessively noisy may have worn bearings and is also prone to fluid leaks. The air conditioning pump mounted on top of the engine can give problems if not regularly used. In the case of V12s, particularly the earlier models with dreadful fuel consumption, many owners just never used the air conditioning as it could take away another valuable 2mpg when in operation. Lack of use easily causes damage to the compressor, which can cost many hundreds of pounds to replace. Air conditioning does not like not being used! Even if you do not like air conditioning the system should be run for half an hour every few months just to help lubricate the compressor.

Of the transmissions fitted, a manual gearbox or the later GM400 automatic transmission are the most robust. Synchromesh on the old manual 4-speed gearbox with overdrive should still be good and first gear should not be noisy. Overdrive was fitted on most early XJs and should operate without hesitation both "in" and "out". The later 5-speed Rover-based box is also relatively strong.

The same automatic transmission problems apply to XJs as to any other car — after all the gearboxes were bought in. The GM400 box is particularly smooth and silky in operation and should always be so. Beware one of these transmissions that is "notchy" during gearchanges, as this indicates that a rebuild will shortly be necessary. Of the earlier transmissions the Borg Warner Model 8s are now quite archaic and some spares are difficult to get. Model 12s are much better whereas the Model 35s and 65/66s are considered at their most stressed in the XJ saloons and can give more trouble. In a lot of cases automatic transmissions really only require a good service, cleaning of the filters and a check on the adjustment of the gear bands.

The choice of tyres for XJs is an important issue. Good quality tyres should always be fitted. As the suspension is so well designed and the handling so superb an XJ encourages spirited use by its driver, and it is not difficult to get over-confident. Unfortunately many people who try to run XJs on a tight budget fit remould tyres, totally inappropriate and sometimes lethal. Whilst on the subject of tyres and wheels, conventional wire wheels are not recommended for use on XJs although the later bolt-on type can be used.

The suspension generally lasts well but, particularly on Series I and II models, front springs sag with age and use, leading to an imbalance in the handling and even fouling of the wheel arches by the tyres. All rubbers, ball joints and mountings on the suspension require regular attention to ensure they are in first-class condition.

The rear suspension is mounted on the usual Jaguar independent rear frame. As the brakes are inboard they are often neglected and if oil has leaked from the differential unit it is bound to have affected the brakes. Rear suspension radius arm mountings rot out very easily and also require regular inspection.

Exhaust systems are a constant irritation. Being difficult to fit they often cause rattles all over the car unless great care is maintained during fitting. Propshaft bearings are prone to failure at regular intervals.

Although mention has already been made of the air conditioning something needs to be said about the normal heating and ventilation system. Jaguar put a lot of effort into the design of the heating system, in some respects over-complicating it. Vacuum pipes can fail very easily on Series I cars and are difficult and fiddly to replace. Series II models have a much more complicated system which is frequently prone to problems but Series III models give less trouble, although the later the model, the more sophisticated the system, especially if it is integrated with air conditioning.

If you are attempting to embark on a major XJ restoration the costs involved could prove prohibitive even if you intend to do most of the work yourself. Series IIs and even some Series Is are unlikely to provide good investment potential for some time to come, and as so many Series IIIs are still around in good condition it is unlikely there is a need to consider restoration of these models. Therefore think carefully. Whilst some remedial work is necessary on most secondhand buys, a major restoration would not be financially viable today.

Before moving on the subject of concours should be reviewed. This has traditionally been the domain (as far as Jaguars are concerned) of the Mark II saloons, E Types and XKs, but as the XJ series will before long become the dominant range in the clubs it is inevitable that they will play an increasing role in concours. At the moment the XJ banner is being carried by literally a handful of XJ owners and there is ample scope for involvement in this field. The degree of preparation to concours standard by XJ owners has rarely been as high as on other models, and now is the time to consider participation.

There is tremendous scope for an XJ owner: in the main the cars are of later date than other models and already one sees A, B and C registered cars in concours events. So you have a good starting point. The difficulty arises in the extent of preparation necessary to be competitive at concours level. The XJ is renowned for its complexity, which in itself presents problems to even the most enthusiastic participant. On a V12 with fuel injection and air conditioning the quantity of pipework under the bonnet is a daunting prospect to clean and prepare. Everything is possible, however, given sufficient time, patience and some knowledge of the cars.

It is a good idea to start with a professional steam clean of the engine bay and the whole underside of the car, but do not be tempted to accept the common practice of lacquering over the cleaned surfaces; this makes it more difficult to keep parts clean and fully presentable for concours. Next comes the systematic cleaning and polishing of every individual item under the bonnet. This may mean removing and disassembling some parts, and here a workshop manual is essential. Some parts may need repainting but always keep to the original finishes —don't be tempted to paint everything in black Hammerite just because it will look good and may last longer! Some concours participants replace many ancillary items, particularly plastic parts, as sometimes these will not clean back to their original state. Such items as under-bonnet sound-deadening materials, wiring and hoses (as well as hose clips) will also need replacing if your car is to be competitive.

A good steam clean of the underside will identify areas of (hopefully) only surface rust and items for repainting and cleaning. Exhausts usually pose a problem as do the front and rear suspension. At the rear, particularly if the XJ is well used or an older model, it may be necessary to remove the subframe and dismantle the suspension and rear axle assembly to clean and repaint. Remember, in the majority of concours events originality is the key to the game. Always re-finish in original colours and finishes.

As for bodywork, assuming the car is already in a good state (it is pointless going to the extremes mentioned above if the bodywork is not properly prepared) thorough cleaning should be all that is required. Remember areas like the insides of wheel-arch lips, the undersides of the valances, door bottoms, and even the bolts that secure the body panels! Needless to say the chromework should be in pristine condition and thorough cleaning is vital around the "egg crate" radiator grilles of Series I XJ6s, the under-bumper air intakes, badges, etc.

The interior will hopefully not need too much work as the XJ series is still relatively young. Carpets may need replacing but beware working on odd pieces of veneered woodwork: it is highly unlikely that you will ever match the factory finish, so a full woodwork refurbishment may be necessary if there is any damage.

Concours participation can be fun but it can also be very disheartening. It is not for the faint hearted but meeting other competitors can lead to good friendships, and the sight of your XJ effectively better than new in many respects can be reward enough for your efforts.

Modifications

Without reading this book most owners will already know that the XJ is a fine motor car. It has won so much acclaim over the years that many people still regard it as the Best Car in the World regardless of price. How therefore can one improve on the very best?

I am a purist and often say that Jaguars should be left as Sir William Lyons intended; after all the factory did all the development work and in the main they got it right, so why depart from the original?

There are, however, aspects that may need improvement either to bring an older model up to later specification or to modify existing specification in the light of newer and more appropriate technology.

First let's look at the bodywork, where there is not a great deal of scope. In the past some have changed the Series I XJ6 radiator grille for a V12 one as they generally look better, and some Series II cars have been modified to Series III specification with the rubber bumpers, later wheels, etc., but as the cars get more valuable this trend will surely disappear. A Coupé suitably resprayed with the vinyl roof removed can look very "different". In the opposite vein, it was the fashion in the seventies to fit vinyl roof coverings to Series II saloons, and properly done with appropriate chrome finishers this can also look good on a Series III. Speaking of Series IIIs, it is possible to fit North American spec. energy-absorbing rubber bumper units with no detraction from originality. These have piston units to absorb impacts at lowspeeds.

Wheels and tyres can easily be interchanged between all the models. The original Kent alloys still used on the Daimler Double Six are not only cheap to purchase new but look good and are easy to maintain. Chromium-plated wheels will enhance the look of any XJ and will take most types of Jaguar hub caps. The later "pepperpot" alloy wheels can also be used on any XJ.

A fashion that many cars including Jaguars seem to be going through involves the fitting of styling kits, which can look very effective on an XJ saloon, particularly a Series III. The kits are fibreglass and usually require spraying to co-ordinate with the car's bodywork colour. The kit usually includes new GRP front and rear bumpers (which in themselves are sculptured with air dams and spoilers) and over-sills. Some kits also include a boot-mounted spoiler.

Colour coding is much in evidence these days and can look appealing on an XJ, like this Coupé prepared by Status Cars of Coventry.

A Jaguar factory mock-up of a body styling kit for an XJ saloon before the arrival of TWR, Arden, etc.

Another body styling kit, one of many now produced for XJs.

The Arden Jaguar, modified and available from the Duncan Hamilton Company.

Autosport Design came up with these proposals for a stylised XJ saloon.

At one time several companies including Lister and Arden were producing modified XJs using body kits; other improvements which could be adopted today include colour-coding of all the brightwork.

There is little that can be done with the interior. Series II seats will fit earlier cars and last better as well as being more comfortable. If you want to go one stage further it is possible to fit Recaro seats, even ones with heated centre panels. Other improvements could include the fitting of rear head restraints to those models not so equipped, the adoption of the electronic trip computer (which would involve some dashboard changes to most cars), air conditioning, and even cruise control to some automatic transmission models. The centre console brightwork can be removed in favour of the later plain black type. The Series II dashboard can be improved by fitting later instruments without the nasty bright surrounds. Nylon over-rugs, a standard fitment on Vanden Plas models, can still be purchased and will fit any other L.W.B. model, and Jaguar still produce fitted rubber over-mats which are a useful and worthwhile addition. Some firms, including Arden, produced special steering wheels in various designs which may still be available. As tinted glass was not always standard on XJs, it is possible to exchange providing the donor car is of the same Series. Whilst perhaps a long-winded procedure, the fitment of tinted glass does have its practical as well as aesthetic advantages.

On the mechanical front a number of improvements can be made. Starting under the bonnet, Series I six-cylinder radiators were generally poor, providing inadequate cooling, and the fitment of a later or V12 radiator will vastly improve matters, as will the fitment of the radiator from an early air-conditioned model. The radiators on Series I six-cylinder cars were also poor and if clogged will soon overheat.

The 2.8-litre engine, as already described, suffered regular piston failure and most have already been replaced by 4.2-litre units. Some Jaguar specialists replaced 2.8-litre engines with 3.4s from S Types or even 420s, these being much stronger engines, thus eliminating the piston problem and at the same time giving improved performance, although some modifications are necessary. This remains a viable option today. Although not original the 4.2-litre unit is far superior and will give improved performance and economy, though the 2.8-litre differential unit should be replaced with the 4.2 unit with its higher axle ratio.

LEFT. The Mark X/420G model can provide a three-carburettor conversion for an XJ unit, though modified air cleaner trunking would be required due to restrictions in room in the engine bay.

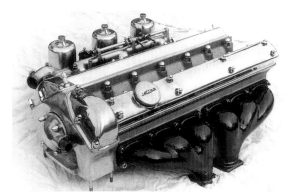

On Series II 4.2-litre engines the carburettors (HA8) can be replaced by Series I HD8, which will give better and smoother performance. These can also be taken from a 420. It is possible to fit a triple-carburettor system from a 420G or Mark X to any 4.2-litre XJ engine; there is space to accommodate the manifold and carburettors and such a change should improve performance considerably. Such items as high-lift camshafts and high-compression pistons can also improve performance. If going to such extremes the later solid-skirt pistons providing an 8.7:1 compression ratio are a good modification on earlier engines. The 4.2 Series III engine with oil cooler is quite a good unit, if perhaps not as long-lived; an oil cooler fitted to any XJ engine will improve matters.

As far as early V12 engines are concerned these can be improved by the fitting of 2in SU carburettors, although underbonnet space could prove a problem. If you don't mind eliminating the air conditioning a good 2mpg saving in fuel consumption can be achieved, as well as making the engine bay easier to work in. The later injection engines are stronger, with a better crankshaft, and run at a lower oil pressure; one of these would be a good idea if your own engine is in a poor state. In addition, the modified digital injection system on pre-HE engines gives better bhp. Overall the post-HE model with Fireball head is superior for a road-going car, not quite so accelerative but with much improved fuel consumption.

ABOVE. The fitment of earlier polished alloy cam covers to an XJ engine, though not original, always looks good.

Companies like K.R.S. can modify a V12 Jaguar engine to unbelievable specification, in this instance with no less than six twin-choke Weber carburettors. This engine is in a Cobra replica.

A highly modified 5-valve cylinder head for the V12 engine can produce some remarkable changes in performance.

An unusual modification for the V12 engine was conceived by Roger Bywater, ex-Jaguar Senior Development Engineer, who in the mid-eighties came up with a "modular engine" to improve fuel economy. The standard V12 engine uses up to three times as much fuel at 30mph as it does at 120mph, and by the intriguing notion of disabling some of the twelve cylinders in low-demand conditions Roger maintained that the remaining operational cylinders would use fuel more efficiently. He found that the idling quality of the V12 running on only six cylinders was improved. Another side-effect was that fewer cylinders produced less exhaust gas.

A specially prepared microelectronic control unit was fitted to control the fuel injection signals as and when 12 cylinders were required. In operation the V12 engine runs on all 12 cylinders when started, to ensure stable operation and good driveaway. For up to 85% of normal journeys the system will allow the engine to run on six cylinders, which can be maintained at up to 85mph on flat roads. The other six cylinders cut in automatically dependent on conditions or by manual switching. Fuel consumption was claimed to be improved by up to 50%.

On the transmission side a manual gearbox is always a better bet for performance and economy, but beware trying to fit a Jaguar manual gearbox to a V12 saloon: it will just not stand the extra torque. Manual gearboxes are getting scarcer but if the opportunity arises it is a good investment to change a 4.2-litre car to manual transmission — only remember you may also have to change the propshaft and rear axle ratio. As far as automatic transmissions are concerned the later the 'box the better. They are interchangeable provided all the ancillaries are also changed. As far as V12s are concerned the latest GM400 is by far the best, although fitting it to an earlier car may necessitate altering the crankshaft.

At the rear the axle ratio can make a marked difference to economy and performance on any XJ. As many Series II and early Series III models were badly geared, changing to a 2.88:1 axle can increase top speed to a genuine 120mph without going into the red on the rev counter, and provide 20mpg.

The steering of all models can be improved by replacing the rack mounting bushes with the heavy duty solid nylon type, giving more precise steering response. On Series I models, the fitment of the later Series II rack will also improve responsiveness but will also necessitate changing the column. Pre-Series III XJs suffered from lack of "feel" from the power steering, and fitting a larger pulley to the steering pump will help.

Brakes on Series Is can be improved by fitting a Series II front axle with four-pot calipers and V12 ventilated discs will also give an improvement in braking on all models, and harder brake pads will reduce fade at the expense of slightly higher pedal pressures.

In the suspension department the use of uprated front springs can improve XJs appreciably, and XJ6s can be fitted with standard V12 springs. Koni adjustable shock absorbers are a must. One of the ultimate Series III XJ conversions is carried out by TWR, who can lower and stiffen the suspension, add a five-speed manual gearbox, and uprate the engine right up to the latest 6-litre XJRS specification – at a price.

There are, I am sure, lots of other minor or major modifications that could be made to an XJ saloon, but as to whether many of these actually make the car better, I am not so sure!

Chronology of model introductions and major changes

September 1986	XJ6 2.8 and 4.2 saloons introduced.
October 1969	Daimler Sovereign 2.8 and 4.2 introduced.
December 1969	Borg Warner Model 12 auto transmission introduced.
July 1972	XJ12 5.3-litre saloon introduced.
August 1972	Daimler Double Six saloon introduced.
September 1972	Daimler Double Six VDP saloon introduced.
October 1972	XJ6L and XJ12L (long-wheelbase models) introduced.
August 1973	Series I XJ production ceased.
September 1973	Series II XJ saloons introduced, all models (except 2.8).
December 1973	Borg Warner Model 65 auto transmission introduced.
April 1975	XJ6C and XJ12C Coupé models introduced.
May 1975	XJ 3.4-litre saloon introduced.
May 1975	Daimler Vanden Plas 4.2-litre saloon introduced.
May 1975	Fuel-injection V12 engine introduced.
April 1977	GM 400 auto transmission introduced.
November 1977	Coupé production ceased.
May 1978	Fuel-injection XJ6 introduced.
March 1979	Series II production ceased.
March 1979	Series III saloons introduced (all models).
September 1981	HE specification V12 engine introduced.
October 1981	New thermo-plastic acrylic paint introduced.
October 1982	Wax injection undersealing introduced.
October 1982	Daimler name dropped in European markets.
October 1982	Jaguar Sovereign models introduced.
August 1983	Vanden Plas production ceased.
May 1987	XJ6 Series III production ceased.
May 1989	All V12 production adapted to unleaded fuel.
January 1990	ABS braking introduced on V12 Series III.
November 1991	Last Jaguar XJ Sovereign produced.
May 1992	Daimler Double Six still in limited production.

Model specifications and technical data

In this section will be found technical specifications of all the models covered in this publication. As far as performance figures are concerned these are taken from contemporary road tests and some figures may vary slightly depending on the actual car tested, weather conditions, etc. Technical specifications cover standard production models only and could vary, as many changes took place during the total period of production.

Jaguar XJ6 2.8-litre saloon/Daimler 2.8-litre Sovereign saloon Series 1

Number of cylinders: 6
Cubic Capacity: 2,792cc
Bore and stroke: 83 × 86mm
Power: 140bhp at 5,500rpm
Torque: 150lb.ft at 4,250rpm
Compression ratio: 8.5:1
Carburation: Twin SU HD8
Transmission: **Manual**, Jaguar 4-speed all-synchromesh with overdrive where specified. Gearbox ratios: 1st 11.99:1, 2nd 7.79:1, 3rd 5.68:1, 4th 4.09:1, reverse 13.81:1. With Laycock overdrive fitted, 1st 13.32:1, 2nd 8.67:1, 3rd 6.33:1, 4th 4.55:1, overdrive 4th 3.54:1, reverse 15.35:1. **Automatic**, Borg Warner Type 35 unit with D-2-1 control. Ratios: top 4.09:1 (with torque converter 8.18:1), intermediate 5.93/11.88:1, low 9.82/19.62:1, reverse 8.38/16.76:1.
Rear axle: Hypoid bevel
Rear axle ratios: 3.31:1 manual transmission without overdrive, 3.54:1 manual transmission with overdrive, 4.09:1 automatic transmission.
Suspension: **Front**, fully independent on subframe attached to body by rubber mountings. Twin wishbones, anti-roll bar. Anti-dive geometry with coil springs and separate dampers with expanded polyurethene damper mountings. **Rear**, fully independent with coil springs mounted within separate subframe with differential.
Wheels and tyres: Pressed steel bolt-on wheels, 6in wide rims, Dunlop low profile SP Sport radial-ply tyres of E70 VR 15 size with anti-aquaplaning tread pattern.

Brakes: Girling disc brakes all round with vacuum servo. Independent circuits to front and rear. Automatic adjustment for wear. Self adjusting handbrake.
Steering: Rack and pinion with power assistance (except standard model). 16in two spoke steering wheel. 3½ turns lock to lock. Turning circle 36ft. Telescopically adjustable steering column, built-in lock with ignition switch.
Fuel tanks: Twin (23 gals total capacity). Electrically operated SU Auf 303 pumps.
Overall length: 189.5in
Overall width: 69.6in
Wheelbase: 108.8in
Track front: 58in
Track rear: 58.6in
Overall height: 52.8in
Ground clearance: 6in
Overall weight (dry): 30.25cwt
Production: Jaguar — From Chassis nos. IG 1001 (rhd) and IG 50001 (lhd), September 1968 to May 1973. Total made 13301 rhd, 6125 lhd, grand total 19426. Daimler Sovereign — Total made 3221.
Performance: **Manual transmission,** 0-50mph 8.2secs, 0-60mph 11secs, 0-100mph 35secs, standing quarter mile 18.1secs, maximum recorded speed 117mph. **Automatic transmission,** 0-50mph 9.3secs, 0-60mph 12.6secs, 0-100mph 39.9secs, standing quarter mile 19.2secs, maximum recorded speed 113mph, average fuel consumption 15-20mpg.

Jaguar XJ6 4.2-litre saloon/Daimler 4.2-litre Sovereign saloon Series 1

Number of cylinders: 6
Cubic capacity: 4,235cc
Bore and stroke: 92.07 × 106mm
Power: 173bhp at 4,750rpm
Torque: 227lb.ft at 3,000rpm
Compression ratio: 8:1 standard, 7:1 or 9:1 optional
Carburation: Twin SU HD8
Transmission: **Manual**, Jaguar 4-speed all-synchromesh with overdrive where specified. Gearbox ratios: 1st 9.7:1, 2nd 6.31:1, 3rd 4.6:1, 4th 3.31:1, reverse 11.17:1. With Laycock overdrive fitted, 1st 10.39:1, 2nd 6.75:1, 3rd 4.91:1, 4th 3.54:1, overdrive 4th 2.76:1, reverse 11.92:1. **Automatic**, Borg Warner Type 35 unit with D-2-1 control. Ratios, top 3.31:1 (with torque converter 6.62:1), intermediate 4.8/9.6:1, low 7.9/15.8:1, reverse 6.92/13.24:1.
Rear axle: Hypoid bevel
Axle Ratios: 3.31:1 manual transmission without overdrive, 3.54:1 manual transmission with overdrive, 3.31:1 automatic transmission.
Suspension: **Front**, fully independent on subframe attached to body by rubber mountings. Twin wishbones, anti-roll bar. Anti-dive geometry with coil springs and separate dampers with expanded polyurethene damper mountings. **Rear**, fully independent with coil springs mounted within separate subframe with differential.

Wheels and tyres: Pressed steel bolt-on wheels, 6in wide rims. Dunlop low profile SP Sport radial-ply tyres of E70 VR 15 size with anti-aquaplaning tread pattern.

Steering: Rack and pinion with power assistance. 16in two spoke steering wheel. 3 ½ turns lock to lock. Turning circle 36ft. Telescopically adjustable steering column, built-in lock with ignition switch.

Fuel tanks: Twin (23 gals total capacity). Electrically operated SU Auf 303 pumps.

Overall length: 189.5in (swb), 194.75in (lwb)

Overall width: 69.6in

Wheelbase: 108.8in (swb), 112.75in (lwb)

Track front: 58in

Track rear: 58.6in

Overall height: 52.8in

Ground Clearance: 6in

Overall weight (dry): 30.75cwt (swb), 34cwt (lwb)

Production: Jaguar — From Chassis nos. 1L 1001 (rhd) and 1L 50001 (lhd) swb cars, 2E 1001 (rhd) and 2E 50001 (lhd) lwb cars, September 1968 (swb) October 1972 (lwb) to July 1973. Total made 33467 rhd (swb), 583 rhd (lwb), 25505 lhd (swb), 1 lhd (lwb), grand total 59556. Daimler Sovereign — Total made 11522 (swb), 396 (lwb).

Performance: **Manual transmission** , 0-50mph 6.6 secs, 0-60mph 8.8secs, 0-100mph 24.1secs,. Standing quarter mile 16.5secs, maximum recorded speed 124mph, average fuel consumption 15mpg. **Automatic transmission** , 0-50mph 7.6secs, 0-60mph 10.1secs, 0-100mph 30.4secs, standing quarter mile 17.5secs, maximum recorded speed 120mph, average fuel consumption 15mpg.

Jaguar XJ12 5.3-litre saloon/Daimler Double Six saloon Series 1

Number of cylinders: 12

Cubic capacity: 5,343cc

Bore and stroke: 90 × 70mm

Power: 253bhp at 6,000rpm

Torque: 302lb.ft at 3,500rpm

Compression ratio: 9:1

Carburation: Four Zenith 175 CDSE

Transmission: Automatic only, Borg Warner 3-speed Model 12. Gear ratios, top 1.0:1 (with torque converter 2.0:1), intermediate 1.45/2.9:1, low 2.40/4.80:1, reverse 2.0/4.0:1.

Rear axle: Salisbury hypoid bevel with Power-Lok limited slip differential

Rear axle ratio: 3.31:1

Suspension: **Front**, fully independent on subframe attached to body by rubber mountings. Twin wishbones, anti-roll bar, anti-dive geometry with coil springs and separate dampers with expanded polyurethane damper mountings. **Rear**, fully independent with coil springs mounted within separate subframe with differential.

Wheels and tyres: Pressed steel ventilated, 6in wide rims with low profile SP Sport Dunlop radial-ply 205 × 70 VR 15 tyres featuring steel breaker and anti-aquaplane tread pattern.

Brakes: Girling disc brakes (ventilated to the front) with vacuum servo. Independent circuits to front and rear. Automatic adjustment for wear. Self adjusting handbrake.

Steering: Rack and pinion with power assistance. 16in two spoke steering wheel. 3 ½ turns lock to lock. Turning circle 36ft. Telescopically adjustable steering column, built in lock with ignition switch.

Fuel tanks: Twin (20 gals total capacity). Electrically operated SU Auf 303 pumps.

Overall length: 189.5in (swb), 194.75in (lwb)

Overall width: 69.6in

Wheelbase: 108.8in (swb), 112.75in (lwb)

Track front: 58in

Track rear: 58.6in

Overall height: 52.8in

Ground clearance: 6in

Overall weight (dry): 35cwt

Production: Jaguar — From July 1972 to August 1973. Total made 720 rhd (swb), 1762 lhd (swb), 750 rhd (lwb), 3 lhd (lwb), grand total 3235. Daimler Sovereign — 466/VDP 342.

Performance: 0-50mph 5.9secs (swb) 6secs (lwb), 0-60mph 7.4secs (swb) 7.8secs (lwb), 0-100mph 19secs (swb) 18.8secs (lwb), standing quarter mile 15.7secs (both wheelbases), maximum recorded speed 147mph, average fuel consumption 11-13mpg.

Jaguar/Daimler Sovereign 3.4-litre Series II saloons

Number of cylinders: 6

Cubic capacity: 3,442cc

Bore and stroke: 83 × 106mm

Power: 161bhp at 5,000rpm

Torque: 189lb.ft at 3,500rpm

Compression ratio: 8.8:1

Carburation: Twin SU 1.75in HS6

Transmission: Jaguar 4-speed with overdrive manual gearbox or Borg Warner Type 35 3-speed automatic transmission. Manual gearbox ratios, 1st 11.45:1, 2nd 6.75:1, 3rd 4.91:1, 4th 3.54:1, overdrive 4th 2.75:1. Automatic transmission ratios, low 4.8/2.4:1, intermediate 2.90/1.45:1, top 2.0/1.0:1.

Rear axle: Hypoid bevel

Rear axle ratio: 3.54:1

Suspension: **Front**, fully independent on subframe attached to body by rubber mountings. Twin wishbones, anti-roll bar. Anti-dive geometry with coil springs and separate dampers with expanded polyurethene damper mountings. **Rear**, fully independent with coil springs mounted within separate subframe with differential.

Wheels and tyres: Pressed steel bolt-on 6in wide rims. Dunlop SP sport radial-ply tyres of E 70 VR 15 size.

Brakes: Girling disc brakes all round with vacuum servo. Independent circuits to front and rear. Automatic adjustment for wear, self adjusting handbrake.

Steering: Rack and pinion with power assistance, 16in two spoke steering wheel. 3 ½ turns lock to lock. Turning circle 36ft. Telescopically adjustable steering column, built-in lock with ignition switch.

Fuel tanks: Twin (20 gals total capacity). Twin SU electric pumps.
Overall length: 194.75in
Overall width: 69.6in
Wheelbase: 112.75in
Track front: 58in
Track rear: 58.6in
Overall height: 52.8in
Ground clearance: 6in
Overall weight: 32cwt
Production: Jaguar — From April 1975 to February 1979. Total made 5004 rhd, 1486 lhd, grand total 6490. Daimler Sovereign — Total made 2347.
Performance: **Manual transmission**, 0-50mph 7.8secs, 0-60mph 10.9secs, 0-100mph 37.9secs, standing quarter mile 18secs, maximum recorded speed 117mph. **Automatic transmission**, 0-50mph 9.2secs, 0-60mph 11.9secs, 0-100mph 38secs, standing quarter mile 18.6secs, maximum recorded speed 115mph, average fuel consumption: 16-17mpg.

Jaguar XJ6 4.2-litre/Daimler Sovereign 4.2-litre Series II saloons

Number of cylinders: 6
Cubic capacity: 4,235cc
Bore and stroke: 92.7 × 106mm
Power: 170bhp at 4,500rpm
Torque: 223lb.ft at 3,500rpm
Compression ratio: 7.8:1
Carburation: Twin SU HS8
Transmission: Jaguar 4-speed all-synchromesh gearbox with overdrive or Borg Warner Model 65 3-speed automatic transmission. Manual gearbox ratios, 1st 10.72:1, 2nd 6.74:1, 3rd 4.92:1, 4th 3.54:1, overdrive 4th 2.94:1. Automatic transmission ratios, low 4.78/2.39:1, intermediate 2.9/1.45:1, top 2.0/1.0:1.
Rear axle: Hypoid bevel
Rear axle ratio: 3.54:1
Suspension: **Front**, fully independent on subframe attached to body by rubber mountings. Twin wishbones, anti-roll bar. Anti-dive geometry with coil springs and separate dampers with expanded polyurethene damper mountings. **Rear**, fully independent with coil springs mounted within separate subframe with differential.
Wheels and tyres: Pressed steel bolt-on wheels, 6in wide rims. Dunlop SP sport radial-ply tyres of E70 VR 15 size with anti-aquaplaning tread pattern.
Brakes: Girling disc brakes ventilated all round with vacuum servo. Independent circuits to front and rear. Automatic adjustment for wear and self adjusting handbrake.
Steering: Rack and pinion with power assistance, 16in two spoke steering wheel. 3½ turns lock to lock. Turning circle 36ft. Telescopically adjustable steering column, built-in lock with ignition switch.
Fuel tanks: Twin (20 gals total capacity). Twin SU electric fuel pumps.
Overall length: 189.5in (swb), 194.75in (lwb)
Overall width: 69.6in
Wheelbase: 108.8in (swb), 112.75in (lwb)
Track front: 58in
Track rear: 58.6in
Overall height: 52.8in
Ground clearance: 6in
Overall weight: (dry) 34cwt
Production: From September 1973 to February 1979 (Nov 1974 swb only). Jaguar — Total made 7463 rhd (swb), 4907 lhd (swb), 26236 rhd (lwb), 24676 lhd (lwb), grand total 63282. Daimler Sovereign — Total made 2431 (swb), 14498 (lwb), 878 (VDP).
Performance: (automatic only): 0-50mph 7.8secs, 0-60mph 10.6secs, 0-100mph 31secs, standing quarter mile 17.6secs, maximum recorded speed 117.5mph, overall fuel consumption 14-17mpg.

Jaguar/Daimler XJ6C 2-door Coupé

Number of cylinders: 6
Cubic Capacity: 4,235cc
Bore and stroke: 92,7 × 106mm
Power: 170bhp at 4,500rpm
Torque: 223lb.ft at 3,500rpm
Compression ratio: 7.8:1
Carburation: Twin SU HS8
Transmission: Jaguar 4-speed manual gearbox with overdrive or Borg Warner 3-speed automatic as Series II saloons, ratios as Series II saloons.
Rear axle: Hypoid bevel
Rear axle ratio: 3.54:1
Suspension front and rear: as Series II saloons
Wheels and tyres: as Series II saloons
Brakes/Steering: as Series II saloons
Fuel tanks: Twin (20 gals capacity). Twin SU electric fuel pumps
Overall length: 189.5in
Overall width: 69.6in
Wheelbase: 109in
Track front: 58in
Track rear: 58.6in
Overall height: 52.8in
Ground clearance: 6in
Overall weight (dry): 33cwt
Production: From September 1973 (launch but not produced) to November 1977. Jaguar — Total made 2606 rhd, 3899 lhd, grand total 6505. Daimler — Total made 1676.
Performance: (automatic only) 0-50mph 7.8secs, 0-60mph 10.6secs, 0-100mph 31secs, standing quarter mile 17.6secs, maximum recorded speed 117mph, average fuel consumption 17mpg.

Jaguar XJ 5.3/Daimler Double Six Series II saloons

Number of cylinders: 12
Cubic capacity: 5,343cc
Bore and stroke: 90 × 70mm
Power: 285bhp at 5,850rpm
Torque: 304(294)lb.ft at 3,500rpm
Compression ratio: 9:1

Carburation: Four Zenith Stromberg 175CD SE until May 1975 when replaced by Lucas Bosch Jetronic fuel injection system.

Transmission: GM 400 3-speed automatic. Gearbox ratios, low 5.95/2.48:1, intermediate 3.55/1.48:1, top 3.07:1.

Rear axle: Hypoid with Power-Lok limitedslip differential

Rear axle ratio: 3.31 or 3.07:1

Suspension: **Front**, fully independent on subframe attached to body by rubber mountings. Twin wishbones with anti-roll bar, anti-dive geometry with coil springs and separate dampers with expanded polyurethene damper mountings. **Rear**, fully independent with coil springs mounted within separate subframe with differential.

Wheels and tyres: Pressed steel bolt-on wheels, 6in wide rims. Dunlop low profile SP Sport radial-ply tyres of E70 VR 15 size with anti-aquaplaning tread pattern.

Brakes: Girling disc brakes ventilated all round with vacuum servo. Independent circuits to front and rear. Automatic adjustment for wear and self adjusting handbrake.

Steering: Rack and pinion with power assistance, 16in two spoke steering wheel. 3 ½ turns lock to lock. Turning circle 36ft. Telescopically adjustable steering column, built-in lock with ignition switch.

Fuel tanks: Twin (20 gals total capacity). Twin SU electric fuel pumps.

Overall length: 194.75in

Overall width: 69.6in

Wheelbase: 112.75in

Track front: 58in

Track rear: 58.6in

Overall height: 52.8in

Ground clearance: 6in

Overall weight (dry): 35cwt

Production: From September 1973 to February 1979. Jaguar — Total made 4157 rhd, 10069lhd, grand total 14226. Daimler Sovereign — Total made 2581, VDP 1711.

Performance: 0-50mph 6secs, 0-60mph 7.8secs, 0-100mph 18.8secs, standing quarter mile 15.7secs, maximum recorded speed 147mph, average fuel consumption 13.2mpg.

Jaguar/Daimler XJ 12C 2-door Coupé

Specification as for XJ12 saloon but overall length 189.5in, wheelbase 108.8in, overall weight (dry) 36cwt.

Production: From September 1973 (launched but not produced) to November 1977. Jaguar — Total made 604 rhd, 1269 lhd, grand total 1873. Daimler — Total made 354.

Performance: 0-50mph 5.9secs, 0-60mph 7.6secs, 0-100mph 18.4secs, standing quarter mile 15.7secs, maximum recorded speed 148mph, average fuel consumption 11.9mpg.

Jaguar XJ6/Daimler Sovereign 4.2-litre Series III saloons

Number of cylinders: 6

Cubic capacity: 4,235cc

Bore and stroke: 92.07 × 106mm

Power: 205bhp at 5,000rpm (176bhp at 4,750rpm USA)

Torque: 236lb.ft at 2,750rpm (219lb.ft at 2,500rpm USA)

Compression ratios: 8.7:1 (7.8:1 USA)

Transmission: Jaguar 5-speed manual all-synchromesh gearbox or Borg Warner Model 65 3-speed automatic transmission. Manual gearbox ratios, 1st 10.99:1, 2nd 6.91:1, 3rd 4.62:1, 4th 3.31:1, 5th 2.76:1. Automatic transmission ratios, low 18.42/7.68:1, intermediate 11.05/4.61:1, top 7.37/3.07:1.

Rear axle: Hypoid bevel

Rear axle ratio: 3.07:1 or 3.31:1

Suspension: **Front**, dependent on subframe attached to body by rubber mountings. Twin wishbones, anti-roll bar, anti-dive geometry with coil springs and separate dampers with expanded polyurethene damper mountings. **Rear**, fully independent with coil springs mounted within separate subframe with differential.

Wheels and tyres: Pressed steel bolt-on wheels, 6in wide rims. Dunlop SP Sport radial-ply tyres of E70 VR 15 size with anti-aquaplaning tread pattern.

Brakes: Girling disc brakes, ventilated front, with vacuum servo. Independent circuits to front and rear. Automatic adjustment for wear and self adjusting handbrake.

Steering: Rack and pinion with power assistance, 16in two spoke steering wheel. 3 ½ turns lock to lock. Turning circle 36ft. Telescopically adjustable steering column, built-in lock with ignition switch.

Fuel tanks: Twin (20 gals total capacity). Twin SU electric fuel pumps.

Overall length: 195.2in

Overall width: 69.7in

Wheelbase: 112.8in

Track front: 58.3in

Track rear: 58.9in

Overall height: 53.5in

Ground clearance: 7in

Overall weight (dry): 35.4cwt

Production: From March 1979 to April 1987. Total made Jaguar 27261, Daimler 20490, grand total 47751.

Performance: **Manual transmission**, 0-50mph 7.7secs, 0-60mph 10.5secs, 0-100mph 28.4secs, standing quarter mile 17.6secs, maximum recorded speed 128mph. **Automatic transmission**, 0-50mph 7.4secs, 0-60mph 9.6secs, 0-100mph 27.8secs, standing quarter mile 17.7secs, maximum recorded speed 116mph, average fuel consumption 15-17mpg.

Jaguar/Daimler XJ6 3.4-litre Series III saloons

Number of cylinders: 6

Cubic capacity: 3,442cc

Bore and stroke: 83 × 106mm

Power: 162bhp at 5,250rpm

Torque: 188lb.ft at 4,000rpm

Compression ratio: 8.4:1

Carburation: Twin SU

Transmission: Jaguar 5-speed all-synchromesh manual gearbox or Borg Warner Model 65 3-speed automatic transmission. Manual gearbox ratios, 1st 11.8:1, 2nd

7.38:1, 3rd 4.94:1, 4th 3.54:1, 5th 2.95:1. Automatic
transmission ratios, low 19.55/8.50:1, intermediate
11.9/5.17:1, top 8.14/3.54:1.
Rear axle: Hypoid bevel
Rear axle ratio: 3.07:1 or 3.31:1
Suspension: Front and rear as 4.2-litre
Wheels and tyres: As 4.2-litre
Steering, brakes, fuel tanks: As 4.2-litre
Dimensions: As 4.2-litre
Overall weight: 34cwt
Production: From March 1979 to April 1987. Numbers
not known.
Performance: Automatic transmission, 0-50mph 8.2secs,
0-60mph 11.7secs, 0-100mph 40.7secs, maximum
recorded speed 113mph, overall fuel consumption
18.4mpg.

Jaguar XJ 5.3-litre/Daimler Double Six Series III saloons

Number of cylinders: 12
Cubic capacity: 5,343cc
Bore and stroke: 90 × 70mm
Power: 299bhp at 5,500rpm
Torque: 318lb.ft at 3,000rpm
Compression ratio: 12.5:1
Carburation: Lucas digital electronic fuel injection.
Transmission: GM 400 3-speed automatic transmission,
ratios as previous V12 models.
Rear axle: Hypoid with Power-Lok limited slip
differential
Rear axle ratio: 2.88:1
Suspension: Front and rear as previous V12 models.
Wheels and tyres: Pressed steel ventilated, 6in wide rims
(or special alloys) with Dunlop D7 215 70 VR 15
radial-ply tyres.
Brakes: As previous V12 models.
Steering, fuel tanks: as previous V12 models.
Dimensions: as 4.2-litre Series III models.
Overall weight: 37.8cwt.
Production: From March 1979 (Vanden Plas terminated
1984). Total made Jaguar 12404 to Sept. '90, Daimler
8926 to Sept '90, VDP 894.
Performance: 0-50mph 6.5secs, 0-60mph 8.1secs,
0-100mph 19secs, standing quarter mile 15.9secs,
maximum recorded speed 142mph, overall fuel
consumption 15.6mpg.

*Unless specifically stated details of Daimler models are exactly as
Jaguar derivatives if known. Performance figures are taken from
contemporary road tests (in some cases averaged). Total
production figures are those supplied by Jaguar Cars and should
include all known cars including prototypes.*

Specialists and clubs

Below is a list of specialists and services who cater for the
Jaguar XJ Series I, II and III models, including Daimlers.
Whilst this information will, we hope, be of assistance to
readers, no recommendation is implied.

Car Sales

For a new or secondhand Jaguar XJ the most likely sources
are the Jaguar franchise dealers across the country.
However, they only normally handle cars of a high value,
with a total mileage below 50,000, and with a service
history.

There are also a few specialist secondhand dealers who
concentrate on the XJ Series, some of whom are listed
below:

Hannah Motors, rear of Russel House, 44/46 Uxbridge
Road, Hampton, Middlesex TW12 3AD/ Tel: 081 941
6123
Suppliers of all types of secondhand XJs

Robert Hughes Classic Cars, Weybridge, Surrey. Tel: 0932
858381.
Specialising in very low mileage or one owner XJs

Spares, repairs, restorations

David Manners, 99 Wolverhampton Road, Oldbury, West
Midlands B69 4RJ. Tel: 021 544 4040.
*New and secondhand spares, remanufactured parts, exhaust
systems, rubbers, etc.*

Barry Hankinson, 15 Copse Cross Street, Ross on Wye,
Herefordshire HR9 5PB. Tel: 0989 65789.
Interior trim items.

Ken Jenkins Jaguar Spares, Unit 4, 2 High Road, Carlton
in Lindrick, Worksop, Notts S81 9ED. Tel: 0909
730754/732219 or 0836 241101.
New and secondhand spares specialist

Colin Webb Jaguar Spares, 31 Elms Drive, Garsington, Oxford. Tel: 086736 8114.
Spares

Straight 6, Gemini House, High Street, Edgware, Middlesex HA8 7ET. Tel: 081 952 4667.
Spares

Classic Spares and Classic Engineering, 501 Southbury Road, Enfield, London EN3 4JW. Tel: 081 805 5534.
Spares

Minters, Brackwell Farm, Winchenton Road, Lower Winchenton, Aylesbury, Bucks. Tel: 0844 291390.
New and secondhand mechanical parts

G. H. Nolan, 1 St Georges Way, London SE15. Tel: 081 701 2785.
Spares

Jaguar Spares Specialists, Paxton Mill, Scaitcliffe Street, Accrington, Lancashire. Tel: 0254 398476.
Spares

Motor Wheel Services, Jeddo Road, Shepherds Bush, London W12 9ED
Bolt on wire wheels.

Olaf P. Lund and Son, 2/26, Anthony Road, Saltley, Birmingham B8 3AA.
New and used spares

Alec Poole Exhausts, Buttermilk Hall, Thame Road, Brill, Bucks HP18 9SB.
Stainless steel exhausts

F.B Components, 35/41 Edgeway Way, Marston, Oxford. Tel: 0865 72464.
Full range of new and remanufactured smaller spares

Norman Motors, 100 Mill Lane, London NW6. Tel: 081 431 0940.
Full range of spare parts

J.P Exhausts, Old School House, Brook Street, Macclesfield, Cheshire SK11 7AW. Tel: 0625 619916.
Stainless steel exhaust systems

J.W. Jag Spares, 3 Holmwood Close, Tuffley, Gloucester. Tel: 0452 21038.
New and secondhand spares and car covers

Baileys UK Limited, 107 Mount Pleasant Road, London NW10 3EH.
Girling, Dunlop, Lockheed brake specialists

Specialised Car Covers, Concours House, Main Street, Burley in Wharfedale, Yorkshire LS29 7JP. Tel: 0843 864646.
Tailored car covers

Wainwrights, 13 Pendra Industrial Estate, Bryncrug Road, Trwyn, Gwynedd, Wales. Tel: 0654 710803.
All parts

Chris Coleman Spares, 17 Devonshire Mews, Chiswick, London W4. Tel: 081 995 9833.
New and secondhand spares

M. & C. Wilkinson, Park Farm, Tethering Lane, Everton, Doncaster, South Yorkshire. Tel: 0777 818061.
New and secondhand spares

Jaguar Enthusiasts' Club Limited, c/o Thelma Brotton, Stoneycroft, Moor Lane, Birdwell, Barnsley, South Yorkshire. Tel: 0226 742829.
Specialist tool remanufacture and spares

Martin Robey Sales Limited, Pool Road, Camp Hill Industrial Estate, Nuneaton CV10 9AE. Tel: 0203 386903.
Remanufactured body panels

The Jag Shop, 303 Goldhawk Road, London W12 8EZ. Tel: 081 748 7824.
Spares

Fibresports, 34/36 Bowlers Croft, Charnes Industrial Estate, Basildon, Essex SS14 3ED. Tel: 0268 527331.
Body styling kits

Duncan Hamilton Ltd, The Square, Bagshot, Surrey. Tel: 0276 71010.
Arden range of body/mechanical improvements

Rob Beere Engineering, Unit 4 Malbern Industrial Estate Greg Street, Stockport, Cheshire. Tel: 061 480 7658.
Engine rebuild specialists

Forward Engineering Ltd, Walsh Lane, Meriden, Coventry CV7 7JY. Tel: 0676 23526.
Engine rebuild specialists

AJ6 Engineering Ltd, 60 Hemshall Road, Bollington, Macclesfield, Cheshire. Tel: 0625 573556.
Engine rebuild/modification specialists

Riverside Carriage Company, Dock Road, Connahs Quay, Deside, Clwyd. Tel: 0244 822789.
Spares specialist

ISP International, Hassop Road, rear of 219 Cricklewood Broadway, London NW2 6RX. Tel: 081 450 0488.
Spares specialist

Midland Wheel Services, 86 Stonebury Avenue, Coventry CV5 7EW. Tel: 0203 461958.
Suppliers of Jaguar-style Pepperpot/Kent alloy wheels

G. W. Bartlett Co, 844 Bath Road, Cranford, Middlesex TW5 9UH. Tel: 081 759 8095.
Upholstery

VIP Chroming, Unit 6, Parnall Road, Fishponds, Bristol, Avon BS16 3JH. Tel: 0272 653408.
Rechroming

Ian D. Martin of Darlington. Tel: 0325 286463.
Woodwork restoration

E. J. Rose. Tel: 0623 24741.
Gearbox repair specialists

A. W. Hannah & Son, Snaith, nr. Goole on Humberside. Tel: 0405 860321.
XJ repairs

Ken Bell, Crooked Timbers, White Hart Lane, Wood Street Village, Guildford, Surrey GU3 3EA. Tel: 0483 235153.
XJ repairs

CF Autos (Colin Ford), 52 Preston Drive, Bexleyheath, Kent DA7 4UQ. Tel: 0322 387929
Repairs

Pat Lacey, Lacey's Garage, Carlton in Lindrick, Worksop, Notts. Tel: 0909 732067.
Restoration/repairs

Suffolk and Turley, Unit 7, Attleborough Fields Industrial Estate, Garrett Street, Nuneaton, Warwickshire. Tel: 0203 381429.
Upholstery restoration and replacement

Replica manufacturers

Heritage Engineering Ltd, 1 North Lodge Cottage, Little Offley, nr. Hitchin, Herts SG5 3BS. Tel: 046276 323.
Manufacturers of C Type and SS100 replica kits (or willbuild)

Steadman Motor Car Co, 5 Foundry lane, Hayle, Cornwall TR27 4HP. Tel: 0736 755016.
Manufacturers of Steadman SS100 replica

Autotune Limited, Unit 1, Riverside Industrial Estate, Rishton, Lancashire. Tel: 0254 886819.
Manufacturers of XK120 replica kits

Clubs

The Daimler and Lanchester Owners' Club, Daimler/ Lanchester House, Church Street, Gamlingay, Sandy, Beds. Tel: 0873 890737.
Although primarily involved with the Daimler andLanchester vehicles of the pre-Jaguar era, there is an increasing membership with XJ cars and a special XJ Register has been set up. Contact Brian Long, 15 Ludlow Road, Earlsdon, Coventry, CV5 6JA. Tel: 0203 677500.
The Club also has a thriving Parts Department and although catering for earlier cars may have several items of interest to Daimler XJ owners.

The Jaguar Car Club, c/o Mrs Susan Bradshaw, Bluntington House, Chaddesley Corbett, Kidderminster, Worcs DY10 4NR. Tel: 0562 83 554.
Although the smallest and most recently formed of the Jaguar clubs the Jaguar Car Club is actively involved with racing (having its own series) and liaises with many other worldwide Jaguar clubs, arranging visits, etc. The club also organises two major Spares Days in the UK in conjunction with the Jaguar Enthusiasts' Club.

The Jaguar Drivers Club Limited, Jaguar House, Stuart Street, Luton, Beds. Tel: Luton 419332.
Oldest of the Jaguar clubs in the UK, the JDC majors on external events including a special XJ Day organised by their XJ Register, specially formed to look after the interests of XJ owners.

The Jaguar Enthusiasts' Club Limited, Sherborne, Mead Road, Stoke Gifford, Bristol BS12 6TS. Tel: 0272 698186.
Currently second largest of the clubs and the fastest growing, the JEC caters for all types of owners but specialises in the spares and DIY side. Regular events are organised including two major Spares Days (in conjunction with the Jaguar Car Club) and the club offers specialist tools and spares remanufacture and a discounted insurance scheme.

There are many other Jaguar/Daimler marque clubs around the world. For further information on these contact the Jaguar Car Club (details above) who will be able to put you in touch with the appropriate organisation.